Scott Foresman
SCIENCE

Series Authors

Dr. Timothy Cooney
Professor of Earth Science and
  Science Education
Earth Science Department
University of Northern Iowa
Cedar Falls, Iowa

Michael Anthony DiSpezio
Science Education Specialist
Cape Cod Children's Museum
Falmouth, Massachusetts

Barbara K. Foots
Science Education Consultant
Houston, Texas

Dr. Angie L. Matamoros
Science Curriculum Specialist
Broward County Schools
Ft. Lauderdale, Florida

Kate Boehm Nyquist
Science Writer and Curriculum Specialist
Mount Pleasant, South Carolina

Dr. Karen L. Ostlund
Professor
Science Education Center
The University of Texas at Austin
Austin, Texas

Contributing Authors

Dr. Anna Uhl Chamot
Associate Professor and
  ESL Faculty Advisor
Department of Teacher Preparation
  and Special Education
Graduate School of Education
  and Human Development
The George Washington University
Washington, D.C.

Dr. Jim Cummins
Professor
Modern Language Centre and
  Curriculum Department
Ontario Institute for Studies in Education
Toronto, Canada

Gale Philips Kahn
Lecturer, Science and Math Education
Elementary Education Department
California State University, Fullerton
Fullerton, California

Vincent Sipkovich
Teacher
Irvine Unified School District
Irvine, California

Steve Weinberg
Science Consultant
Connecticut State
  Department of Education
Hartford, Connecticut

Scott Foresman

Editorial Offices: Glenview, Illinois · Parsippany, New Jersey · New York, New York
Sales Offices: Parsippany, New Jersey · Duluth, Georgia · Glenview, Illinois
Carrollton, Texas · Ontario, California
www.sfscience.com

Content Consultants

Dr. J. Scott Cairns
National Institutes of Health
Bethesda, Maryland

Jackie Cleveland
Elementary Resource Specialist
Mesa Public School District
Mesa, Arizona

Robert L. Kolenda
Science Lead Teacher, K-12
Neshaminy School District
Langhorne, Pennsylvania

David P. Lopath
Teacher
The Consolidated School District
of New Britain
New Britain, Connecticut

Sammantha Lane Magsino
Science Coordinator
Institute of Geophysics
University of Texas at Austin
Austin, Texas

Kathleen Middleton
Director, Health Education
ToucanEd
Soquel, California

Irwin Slesnick
Professor of Biology
Western Washington University
Bellingham, Washington

Dr. James C. Walters
Professor of Geology
University of Northern Iowa
Cedar Falls, Iowa

Multicultural Consultants

Dr. Shirley Gholston Key
Assistant Professor
University of Houston-Downtown
Houston, Texas

Damon L. Mitchell
Quality Auditor
Louisiana-Pacific Corporation
Conroe, Texas

Classroom Reviewers

Kathleen Avery
Teacher
Kellogg Science/Technology
Magnet
Wichita, Kansas

Margaret S. Brown
Teacher
Cedar Grove Primary
Williamston, South Carolina

Deborah Browne
Teacher
Whitesville Elementary School
Moncks Corner, South Carolina

Wendy Capron
Teacher
Corlears School
New York, New York

Jiwon Choi
Teacher
Corlears School
New York, New York

John Cirrincione
Teacher
West Seneca Central Schools
West Seneca, New York

Jacqueline Colander
Teacher
Norfolk Public Schools
Norfolk, Virginia

Dr. Terry Contant
Teacher
Conroe Independent
School District
The Woodlands, Texas

Susan Crowley-Walsh
Teacher
Meadowbrook Elementary School
Gladstone, Missouri

Charlene K. Dindo
Teacher
Fairhope K-1 Center/Pelican's
Nest Science Lab
Fairhope, Alabama

Laurie Duffee
Teacher
Barnard Elementary
Tulsa, Oklahoma

Beth Anne Ebler
Teacher
Newark Public Schools
Newark, New Jersey

Karen P. Farrell
Teacher
Rondout Elementary School District
#72
Lake Forest, Illinois

Anna M. Gaiter
Teacher
Los Angeles Unified School District
Los Angeles Systemic Initiative
Los Angeles, California

Federica M. Gallegos
Teacher
Highland Park Elementary
Salt Lake School District
Salt Lake City, Utah

Janet E. Gray
Teacher
Anderson Elementary - Conroe ISD
Conroe, Texas

Karen Guinn
Teacher
Ehrhardt Elementary School - KISD
Spring, Texas

Denis John Hagerty
Teacher
Al Ittihad Private Schools
Dubai, United Arab Emirates

Judith Halpern
Teacher
Bannockburn School
Deerfield, Illinois

Debra D. Harper
Teacher
Community School District 9
Bronx, New York

Gretchen Harr
Teacher
Denver Public Schools - Doull School
Denver, Colorado

Bonnie L. Hawthorne
Teacher
Jim Darcy School
School Dist #1
Helena, Montana

Marselle Heywood-Julian
Teacher
Community School District 6
New York, New York

Scott Klene
Teacher
Bannockburn School 106
Bannockburn, Illinois

Thomas Kranz
Teacher
Livonia Primary School
Livonia, New York

Tom Leahy
Teacher
Coos Bay School District
Coos Bay, Oregon

Mary Littig
Teacher
Kellogg Science/Technology
Magnet
Wichita, Kansas

Patricia Marin
Teacher
Corlears School
New York, New York

Susan Maki
Teacher
Cotton Creek CUSD 118
Island Lake, Illinois

Efraín Meléndez
Teacher
East LA Mathematics Science
Center LAUSD
Los Angeles, California

Becky Mojalid
Teacher
Manarat Jeddah Girls' School
Jeddah, Saudi Arabia

Susan Nations
Teacher
Sulphur Springs Elementary
Tampa, Florida

Brooke Palmer
Teacher
Whitesville Elementary
Moncks Corner, South Carolina

Jayne Pedersen
Teacher
Laura B. Sprague
School District 103
Lincolnshire, Illinois

Shirley Pfingston
Teacher
Orland School Dist 135
Orland Park, Illinois

Teresa Gayle Rountree
Teacher
Box Elder School District
Brigham City, Utah

Helen C. Smith
Teacher
Schultz Elementary
Klein Independent School District
Tomball, Texas

Denette Smith-Gibson
Teacher
Mitchell Intermediate, CISD
The Woodlands, Texas

Mary Jean Syrek
Teacher
Dr. Charles R. Drew Science
Magnet
Buffalo, New York

Rosemary Troxel
Teacher
Libertyville School District 70
Libertyville, Illinois

Susan D. Vani
Teacher
Laura B. Sprague School
School District 103
Lincolnshire, Illinois

Debra Worman
Teacher
Bryant Elementary
Tulsa, Oklahoma

Dr. Gayla Wright
Teacher
Edmond Public School
Edmond, Oklahoma

Activity and Safety Consultants

Laura Adams
Teacher
Holley-Navarre Intermediate
Navarre, Florida

Dr. Charlie Ashman
Teacher
Carl Sandburg Middle School
Mundelein District #75
Mundelein, Illinois

Christopher Atlee
Teacher
Horace Mann Elementary
Wichita Public Schools
Wichita, Kansas

David Bachman
Consultant
Chicago, Illinois

Sherry Baldwin
Teacher
Shady Brook
Bedford ISD
Euless, Texas

Pam Bazis
Teacher
Richardson ISD
   Classical Magnet School
Richardson, Texas

Angela Boese
Teacher
McCollom Elementary
Wichita Public Schools USD #259
Wichita, Kansas

Jan Buckelew
Teacher
Taylor Ranch Elementary
Venice, Florida

Shonie Castaneda
Teacher
Carman Elementary, PSJA
Pharr, Texas

Donna Coffey
Teacher
Melrose Elementary - Pinellas
St. Petersburg, Florida

Diamantina Contreras
Teacher
J.T. Brackenridge Elementary
San Antonio ISD
San Antonio, Texas

Susanna Curtis
Teacher
Lake Bluff Middle School
Lake Bluff, Illinois

Karen Farrell
Teacher
Rondout Elementary School,
   Dist. #72
Lake Forest, Illinois

Paul Gannon
Teacher
El Paso ISD
El Paso, Texas

Nancy Garman
Teacher
Jefferson Elementary School
Charleston, Illinois

Susan Graves
Teacher
Beech Elementary
Wichita Public Schools USD #259
Wichita, Kansas

Jo Anna Harrison
Teacher
Cornelius Elementary
Houston ISD
Houston, Texas

Monica Hartman
Teacher
Richard Elementary
Detroit Public Schools
Detroit, Michigan

Kelly Howard
Teacher
Sarasota, Florida

Kelly Kimborough
Teacher
Richardson ISD
   Classical Magnet School
Richardson, Texas

Mary Leveron
Teacher
Velasco Elementary
Brazosport ISD
Freeport, Texas

Becky McClendon
Teacher
A.P. Beutel Elementary
Brazosport ISD
Freeport, Texas

Suzanne Milstead
Teacher
Liestman Elementary
Alief ISD
Houston, Texas

Debbie Oliver
Teacher
School Board of Broward County
Ft. Lauderdale, Florida

Sharon Pearthree
Teacher
School Board of Broward County
Ft. Lauderdale, Florida

Jayne Pedersen
Teacher
Laura B. Sprague School
District 103
Lincolnshire, Illinois

Sharon Pedroja
Teacher
Riverside Cultural
   Arts/History Magnet
Wichita Public Schools USD #259
Wichita, Kansas

Marcia Percell
Teacher
Pharr, San Juan, Alamo ISD
Pharr, Texas

Shirley Pfingston
Teacher
Orland School Dist #135
Orland Park, Illinois

Sharon S. Placko
Teacher
District 26, Mt. Prospect
Mt. Prospect, IL

Glenda Rall
Teacher
Seltzer Elementary
USD #259
Wichita, Kansas

Nelda Requenez
Teacher
Canterbury Elementary
Edinburg, Texas

Dr. Beth Rice
Teacher
Loxahatchee Groves
   Elementary School
Loxahatchee, Florida

Martha Salom Romero
Teacher
El Paso ISD
El Paso, Texas

Paula Sanders
Teacher
Welleby Elementary School
Sunrise, Florida

Lynn Setchell
Teacher
Sigsbee Elementary School
Key West, Florida

Rhonda Shook
Teacher
Mueller Elementary
Wichita Public Schools USD #259
Wichita, Kansas

Anna Marie Smith
Teacher
Orland School Dist. #135
Orland Park, Illinois

Nancy Ann Varneke
Teacher
Seltzer Elementary
Wichita Public Schools USD #259
Wichita, Kansas

Aimee Walsh
Teacher
Rolling Meadows, Illinois

Ilene Wagner
Teacher
O.A. Thorp Scholastic Acacemy
Chicago Public Schools
Chicago, Illinois

Brian Warren
Teacher
Riley Community Consolidated
   School District 18
Marengo, Illinois

Tammie White
Teacher
Holley-Navarre
   Intermediate School
Navarre, Florida

Dr. Mychael Willon
Principal
Horace Mann Elementary
Wichita Public Schools
Wichita, Kansas

Inclusion Consultants

Dr. Eric J. Pyle, Ph.D.
*Assistant Professor, Science
   Education*
Department of Educational Theory
   and Practice
West Virginia University
Morgantown, West Virginia

Dr. Gretchen Butera, Ph.D.
*Associate Professor, Special
   Education*
Department of Education Theory
   and Practice
West Virginia University
Morgantown, West Virginia

Bilingual Consultant

Irma Gomez-Torres
Dalindo Elementary
Austin ISD
Austin, Texas

Unit A
Life Science

Unit B
Physical Science

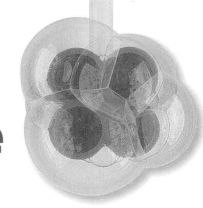

Unit C
Earth Science

Chapter 3
The Sky　C46

Unit D
Human Body

Your Science Handbook

Using Scientific Methods for Science Inquiry

Scientists use scientific methods to find answers to questions. Scientific methods have the steps shown on these pages. Scientists sometimes use the steps in different order. You can use these steps for your own science inquiries.

Problem

The problem is the question you want to answer. Inquiry has led to many discoveries in science. Ask your question.

> Do seeds grow better in soil or in sand?

Give your hypothesis.

Tell what you think the answer is to the problem.

If you plant seeds in soil, they will grow better than seeds planted in sand. ▶

Control the variables.

Change one thing when you test your hypothesis. Keep everything else the same.

> I will put the same amount of water in each cup.

Test your hypothesis.

Do experiments to test your hypothesis. You may need to do experiments more than one time to see if the results are the same each time.

◀ Observe the seeds and compare how they grow.

Collect your data.

Collect data about the problem. Record your data on a chart. You might make drawings or write words or sentences.

Tell your conclusion.

Compare your results and hypothesis. Decide if your hypothesis is right or wrong. Tell what you decide.

Seeds planted in soil grow better than seeds planted in sand.

❓ Inquire Further

Use what you learn to answer other problems or questions. You may want to do your experiment again or change your experiment.

Does the amount of water affect how plants grow? ▶

Using Process Skills for Science Inquiry

Scientists use process skills to do research. You will use process skills when you do the activities in this book.

When you test something, you use process skills. When you collect data, you use process skills. When you make conclusions and tell what you learn, you use process skills.

I hear a high sound

Observing
Your senses are seeing, hearing, smelling, touching, and tasting. Use your senses to find out about objects or things that happen.

Communicating
Use words, pictures, charts, or graphs to share what you learn.

Classifying
Sort or group objects by their properties.

Estimating and Measuring
Estimate means to tell what you think an object's measurement is. Make an estimate. Then measure the object.

Inferring
Make a conclusion or a guess from what you observe or from what you already know.

Predicting

Tell what you think will happen.

Making Definitions

Use what you already know to describe
something or tell what it means.

Making and Using Models

Make a model to show what
you know about something.

Giving Hypotheses

Make a statement you can test
to answer a problem or question.

Collecting Data

Record what you observe and measure.
Use graphs, charts, pictures, or words.
Use what you learned to answer
problems or questions.

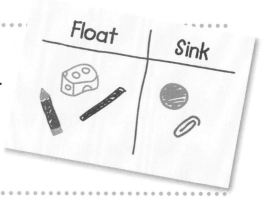

Controlling Variables

Change one thing that may affect what
happens. Keep everything else the same.

Experimenting

Plan and do an investigation to test
a hypothesis or to answer a problem.
Then make conclusions.

? Science Inquiry

As you use your science book, you will ask questions, do investigations, answer your questions, and then tell others what you learned. This is called science inquiry. You can use science inquiry to do this science project.

1 **Ask a question about living things, objects, or things that happen.**

What objects are lighter than an apple?

What objects are lighter than an apple?

2 **Plan and do a simple investigation to answer your question.**

Put an apple on one side of a pan balance. Put another object on the other side. Observe to see which object is lighter.

3 **Use some simple materials and tools to help you.**

Use a pan balance to compare the weight of the objects. Use a chart to show which objects are lighter than the apple.

4 **Use what you observed to answer your question.**

Which objects are lighter than an apple?

5 **Share your information with your class.**

You can use a chart, words, or pictures.

Unit A
Life Science

Science and Technology
In Your World!

Why do some zoos have fake trees?

Branches pop out of the trunks of the fake trees. Giraffes get the exercise they need by walking from tree to tree to eat real food from the fake branches.

Chapter 1
Plants

Can animals make movies?

Yes! This seal wears a video camera on its back. It takes pictures that show scientists what animals do under water.

Chapter 2
Animals

What is a virtual aquarium?

It is a fish tank you can design on a computer. A website lets you choose fish and a habitat. Then your aquarium shows up on the screen.

Chapter 3
Where Plants and Animals Live

Chapter 1
Plants

Plant a Little Seed

♪ Sing to the tune of *I've Been Working on the Railroad*.

Plant a seed and see what happens.
You will be surprised.

In the ground, the roots are growing,
But they're hidden from your eyes.

A stem will soon be growing upward
Reaching for the sky.

From the stem the leaves are growing.
Soon a flower may catch your eye.

First there's a seed.

Then there are roots.

Then come a stem, leaves and a flower.

Plant a little seed.

Plant a little seed.

Plant a seed and watch it grow!

Original lyrics by Gerri Brioso and Richard Freitas.
Produced by Children's Television Workshop.

Learning Science Words

Find the word on this page with yellow behind it. This is a special science word.

Now read the sentence. The sentence tells you what the science word means.

Roots hold the plant in the ground.

Look at page A8. What special science words do you see?

—— roots

When you see a science word in this book, write it on a card. Draw a picture to show the word. Keep the word cards in your desk or in a special folder.

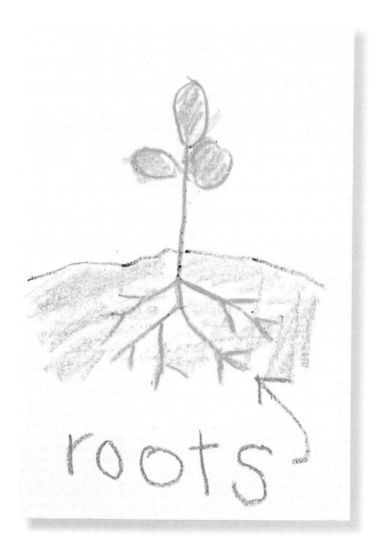

roots

Turn the page to learn more science words.

Turn the page.

What do the roots and stem do?

It is a windy day. Hold onto your hat, or it might blow away! What keeps a plant from blowing away?

Plants have roots. **Roots** hold the plant in the ground. Find the roots in the picture. How does the root of the carrot look different from the other roots?

Roots take in water, too. Where does the water go? It goes to the stem. The **stem** takes the water to other parts of the plant.

Observe roots.

Materials

 plant cup of water foil

crayon tape

Steps

1. Put a plant in the cup.

2. Add water to cover the roots.

3. Cover the top of the jar with the foil.

4. Mark how high the water is.

5. **Observe** the jar every day.

Share. Draw the plant and water when you start and after five days.

Lesson Review

1. What do the roots do?

2. What does the stem do?

3. **Tell** what happened to the water in the cup.

How does water move through plants?

Process Skills

- predicting
- observing

Materials

 cup of water   food color   celery

paper towel

Steps

1. Put a little water in a cup.

2. Add 10 drops of food color.

3. Put the celery into the cup. Stir.

4. Draw what you **predict** will happen.

5. **Observe** the celery the next day. Break the celery. Draw what happened.

Draw what you predict will happen.

Draw what happened.

Think About Your Results

1. What happened to the water?

2. How does the colored water get to the leaves?

 Inquire Further

With what other plants could you try this activity?

What do leaves do?

It is a sunny summer day. You can sit under a shady tree. Look up and see all the leaves!

Leaves are an important part of a plant. Leaves use sunlight, air, and water to make food for the plant.

Leaves come in many shapes and sizes. Some are pointed. Others are round. Some are smaller than your fingernail. Others are bigger than your hand. What kinds of leaves have you seen?

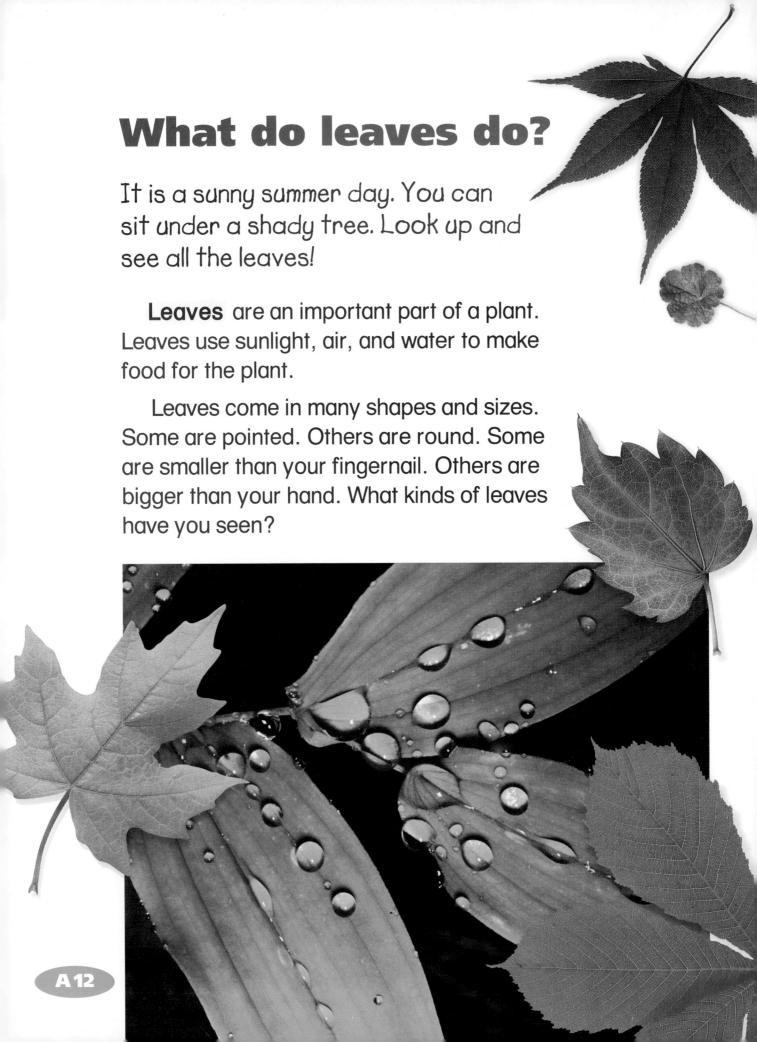

Make a leaf rubbing.

Materials

 paper crayon without wrapper

leaf

Process Skills

- observing

Steps

1. Put a leaf between two pieces of paper.

2. Rub the side of the crayon over the leaf.

3. **Observe** the leaf rubbing.

Share. See if a friend can guess which leaf you used for your rubbing.

Lesson Review

1. What do the leaves do?

2. What are some leaf shapes?

3. **Tell** what your leaf rubbing looks like.

How does a seed grow into a plant?

Dig a hole. Plant a seed. What happens to the seed in the ground?

A **seed** can grow into a new plant. This picture shows a bean seed. Water in the soil helps the seed coat come off. Next, a root grows down. A stem grows up. Leaves grow.

The seed has grown into a bean plant. The new plant needs sunlight, air, and water to grow.

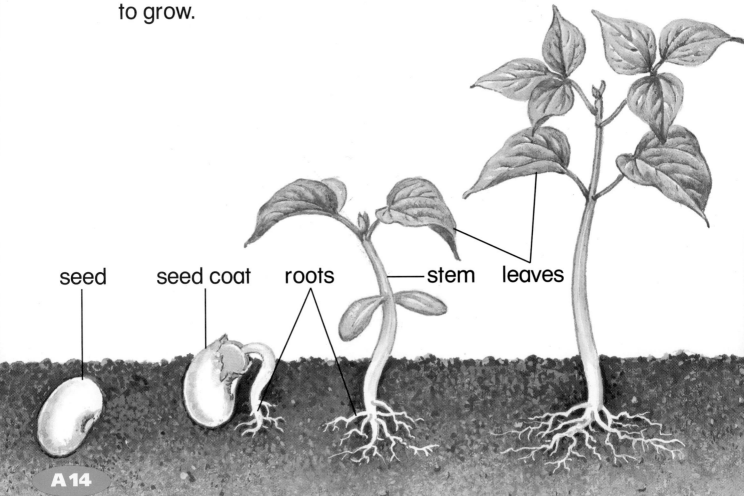

seed   seed coat   roots   stem   leaves

Grow a plant.

Materials

seeds   plastic bag   paper towel

cup of water   soil   stapler

Process Skills

- observing

Steps

1. Put 3 seeds in the bag.

2. Put a little water in the bag.

3. Close the bag.

4. **Observe** the seeds as they grow.

5. When the seeds grow roots, choose one plant. Put it in a cup of soil.

Share. Draw your plant as it grows.

Lesson Review

1. Does the root grow up or down?

2. What does a plant need to grow?

3. **Show** how a plant grows from a seed. Act it out.

How does an apple grow?

Mmm! Bite into a juicy apple. Did you know the apple started as a flower?

In spring, the apple tree is covered with green leaves and flowers.

The petals fall off the flower. An apple begins to form.

Can you find the tiny apple? The apple is a **fruit**. The fruit grows all summer.

In the fall the apple is ripe. It is ready to eat! Look at the cut apple. Find the seeds inside.

Lesson Review

1. What is an apple?

2. What is inside an apple?

3. **Draw** pictures to show how an apple grows.

Experiment with plant growth.

Process Skills

Process Skills

- experimenting
- observing

Materials

 2 plants in containers

 water

 index cards

Problem

How does water affect how plants grow?

Give Your Hypothesis

If you water one plant but not the other, what will happen? Tell what you think.

water   no water

Control the Variables

Put both plants in the same place.

Test Your Hypothesis

Follow these steps to do the **experiment**.

1. Label one plant **water.** Water this plant when the soil feels dry.

2. Label the other plant **no water.** Do not water this plant.

3. **Observe** the plants every day.

Collect Your Data

Use a chart like this one. Draw pictures to show the plants on each day.

Tell Your Conclusion

Compare your results and hypothesis. How does water affect how plants grow?

Inquire Further

What will happen if you give a plant too much water?

What parts of plants do you eat?

Would you like to eat leaves for lunch? When you eat lettuce or spinach, you are eating leaves!

People eat parts of plants. When you eat a carrot, you are eating a root. Part of the broccoli you eat is a stem. Asparagus is a stem too. Peas, corn, and nuts are seeds. Apples and oranges are fruits.

What plant parts do you see in this picture?

Classify the plants you eat.

Materials

 pictures of foods

paper

glue

Process Skills

- classifying

Process Skills

Steps

1 Write the word **roots** on one paper. Do the same thing for **stems, leaves, fruit,** and **seeds.**

2 Gather pictures of foods. Decide what plant part each picture shows.

3 Classify the pictures. Glue them onto the correct papers.

Share. Tell what plant parts you like to eat.

Lesson Review

1. What roots can you eat?

2. What leaves can you eat?

3. Draw a picture of your lunch. Tell if it has a root, stem, leaf, fruit, or seed.

roots

stems

leaves

fruit

seeds

A21

How do people use plants?

Think about your favorite jeans. They are made of cotton. Did you know cotton comes from a plant?

Rope and straw baskets come from plants too. People use wood from trees to make furniture and other things. What do you know that is made of wood?

This forester is planting new trees. When they are big, some will be cut down and made into paper or other things.

Classify objects made from plants.

Materials

   classroom objects

 two cards

Process Skills

- classifying

Process Skills

Steps

1. Write **from plants** on one card.
   Write **not from plants** on another card.

2. Gather some objects. Which are from plants? Which are not from plants?

3. Classify the objects into the two groups.

Share. What did you use today that is from a plant?

Lesson Review

1. What is paper made from?

2. What plant do people use to make jeans?

3. **Draw** an object that comes from a plant. Draw an object that does not come from a plant.

Chapter 1 Review

Reviewing Science Words

1. What do the **roots** do?

2. What does the **stem** do?

3. What do **leaves** do?

4. Tell how a **seed** grows into a plant.

5. Name one kind of **fruit** .

Reviewing Science Ideas

1. What root, stem, leaf, seed, and fruit can you eat? Make a list.

2. Name three things people make from plants.

Make a poster of a plant.

Materials

drawing paper   crayons or markers

1. Draw a plant. Label the parts.
2. Name your plant.
3. Tell what your plant needs to stay alive.
4. Tell how people might use your plant.
5. Share your poster with others.

Chapter 2
Animals

All Kinds of Animals

♪ Sing to the tune of *Oh, Susanna.*

There are animals of many kinds,
They can be short or tall.
Most animals have legs that bend
But some have none at all.

Hippopotami have short fat legs
Giraffes' are tall and thin.
And if they run a race today,
Who do you think would win?

Animals are travelers.
There are lots of reasons why.
With feathers, fins or scales or feet,
They walk, slither, swim, or fly.

Original lyrics by Gerri Brioso and Richard Freitas.
Produced by Children's Television Workshop.
Copyright ©1999 Sesame Street, Inc.

A27

Reading a Science Activity

Look at the activity about animals. Point to the title. Look at the picture. What materials do you need? Do the steps in order.

Here is the title. ——

Here are the materials. ⤹

Here are the steps. ——

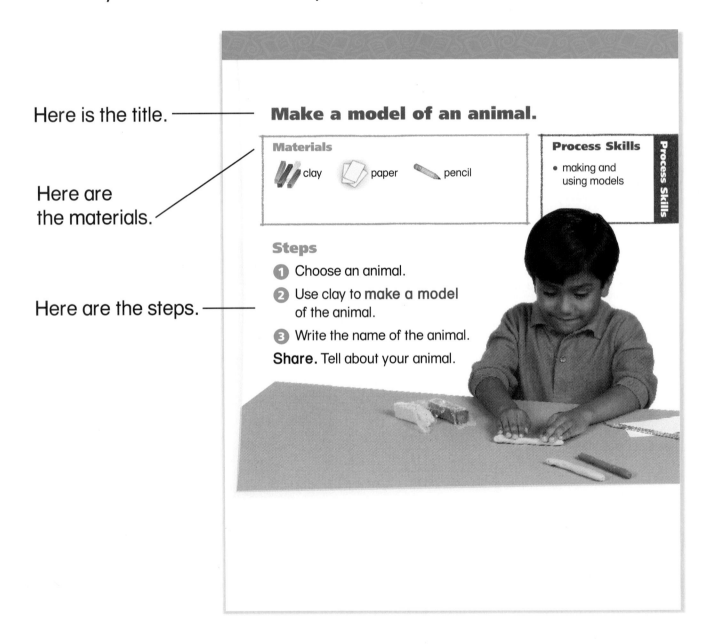

Make a model of an animal.

Materials

clay   paper   pencil

Process Skills

- making and using models

Process Skills

Steps

1 Choose an animal.
2 Use clay to **make a model** of the animal.
3 Write the name of the animal.
Share. Tell about your animal.

Make a model of an animal.

Materials

clay   paper   pencil

Process Skills

- making and using models

Steps

1. Choose an animal.

2. Use clay to **make a model** of the animal.

3. Write the name of the animal.

Share. Tell about your animal.

Turn the page.

Turn the page to read a lesson and an activity.

What kinds of animals are there?

Look up! A bird is flying. Look down! A frog is hopping by. Animals are everywhere!

Animals come in many sizes. What is the biggest animal you can think of? What is the smallest?

Animals come in many shapes and colors. Tell about the shape of the fish. Find an animal that has bright colors. What else can you tell about animals?

Classify animals.

Materials

 animal pictures

2 pieces of paper

Process Skills

- classifying
- communicating (tell)

Process Skills

Steps

1. **Classify** the pictures into two groups.

2. Have a friend **tell** how you grouped the pictures.

3. Take turns. Do it again.

Share. Tell how you classified the pictures.

Lesson Review

1. Name a big animal.

2. Name a small animal.

3. **Tell** another way to classify the animal pictures.

How do animals move?

Do you like to skip or run? Do you like to jump or crawl?

Animals move in many ways too. A dog uses legs to walk or run. A monkey uses arms and legs to climb and swing in trees.

Snakes and fish have no legs. A snake slithers on the ground. A fish uses fins to swim. What does a duck use to swim?

How does this frog move? Can you move in that way?

Move like an animal.

Materials

 animal cards

Process Skills

• observing

Process Skills

Steps

1 Work with a group.

2 Choose an animal card.

3 Move like the animal.

4 Have the group **observe** and guess the animal.

Share. Name an animal that can move in more than one way.

Lesson Review

1. Name four ways animals move.

2. What parts of animals help them move?

3. **Draw** a picture that shows an animal moving.

What coverings do animals have?

Brrr! It is a cold day. How do you stay warm?

A tiger is covered with fur. Fur keeps the tiger warm. A bird's feathers keep heat in and water out.

Coverings help animals in other ways. The scales on a fish are slippery. They help the fish swim. How do you think a shell helps a turtle?

Find fur, feathers, scales, and a shell in the pictures. Which animal matches each covering?

Observe a feather.

Materials

 feather

 hand lens

Process Skills

- communicating (write)
- observing

Steps

1. Touch the feather. Feel all the parts.

2. Write how the feather feels.

3. Use a hand lens. Observe the feather.

4. Draw the feather.

Share. Tell how parts of the feather are different.

Lesson Review

1. Name four animal coverings.

2. How can fur help animals?

3. Tell how feathers help birds.

What is an insect?

They creep! They crawl! They fly! What do you think they are? They are insects.

beetle

An **insect** is an animal. All insects have three main body parts. These body parts are called the **head**, **thorax**, and **abdomen**. Find the body parts of the ant.

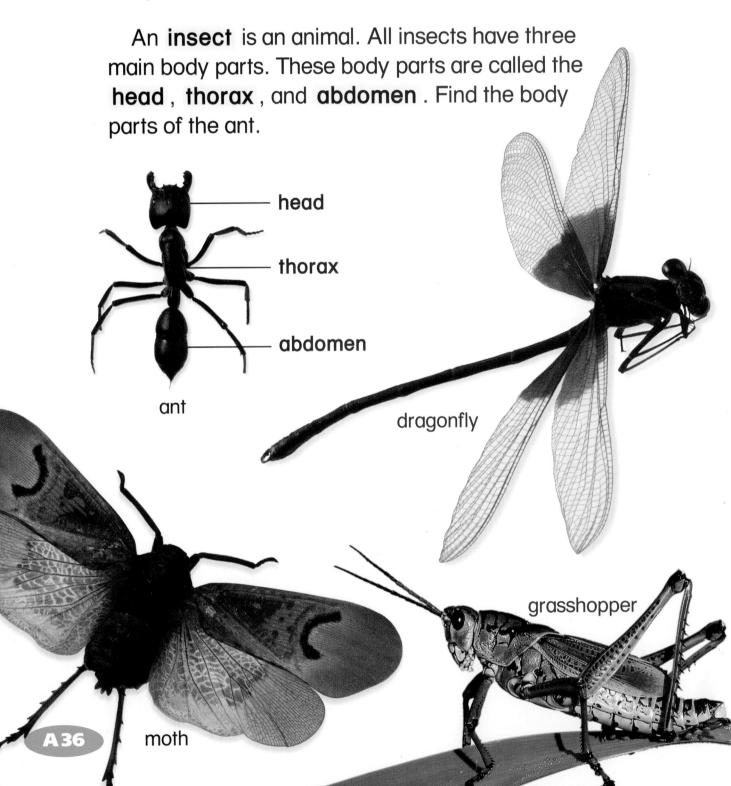

head

thorax

abdomen

ant

dragonfly

grasshopper

moth

mantis

butterfly

wasp

Find the picture of the wasp. How many legs does it have? All insects have six legs.

Lesson Review

1. Name the three main body parts of an insect.

2. How many legs does an insect have?

3. **Tell** the names of some insects.

What are the parts of an ant?

Process Skills

- observing
- making and using models

Process Skills

Materials

 safety goggles

clay

pipe cleaners

Steps

1. Put on your safety goggles.

2. **Observe** the picture of the ant.

3. **Make a model.** Shape clay into three main body parts.

4. Stick the parts together.

5. Add pipe cleaners for legs.

6. Add other body parts.

Think About Your Results

1. How is your model like a real ant?

2. How is your model different from a real ant?

 **Inquire Further**

What are some other insect body parts?

What do animals need?

A snake, a skunk, a snail, and a spider all need the same things. What do they need?

All animals need food and water. This bird gets food and water by eating berries. Where else can it find water?

The spider catches insects in a web. The spider gets food and water by eating insects.

Animals also need air and a place to live. Pets live with people. The spider lives in a web. Where else do animals live?

Lesson Review

1. What four things do animals need?

2. Where do some animals live?

3. **Tell** how a spider gets food and water.

What are baby animals like?

A baby leopard is called a cub. How does a leopard take care of its cub?

Some baby animals need care from their parents. A **parent** is a mother or father. The leopard licks its baby to keep it clean. The bird brings food to its babies. How do other animals care for their babies?

A tadpole is a baby frog. A tadpole does not need care from its parents. Find the picture of the tadpole. How does it look different from its parent?

Lesson Review

1. Name an animal that does not need care from its parents.

2. List two ways that animals take care of their babies.

3. **Draw** a baby animal and a parent that look different from each other.

Chapter 2 Review

Reviewing Science Words

1. How many legs does an **insect** have?
2. Draw a picture of an insect. Point to the **head** , **thorax** , and **abdomen** .
3. What is a **parent** ?

Reviewing Science Ideas

1. Name four ways that animals move.
2. Name two animal coverings.
3. Name four things that animals need.
4. What are some ways that animals take care of their babies?

Make an animal mask.

Materials

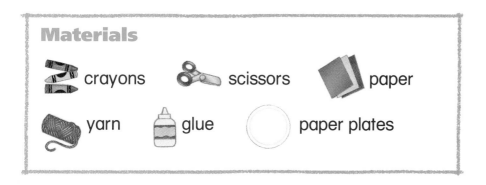

crayons   scissors   paper

yarn   glue   paper plates

1. Make an animal face on your paper plate.
2. Wear your mask. Move like your animal.
3. Make the sounds your animal makes.
4. Tell what your animal needs.

Chapter 3

Where Plants and Animals Live

The Right Habitat

♪ Sing to the tune of *My Bonnie Lies over the Ocean.*

The lizard lives out in the desert.

Around him the cacti grow tall.

It's sunny and dry every day there,

A habitat fit for them all.

The octopus lives in the ocean.
It finds things on which it can dine.
Shrimp, clams, crabs, mussels,
and sea snails,
That habitat suits it just fine.

Habitats, habitats,
Habitats have what they need to live.
Habitats, habitats,
Habitats have what they need.

Original lyrics by Gerri Brioso and Richard Freitas.
Produced by Children's Television Workshop.
Copyright ©1999 Sesame Street, Inc.

A47

Tallying

| This is a tally mark. It means 1.

₭₭₭ These tally marks mean 5.

This chart shows how many animals are in the tree.

Animals	Tally	Total
Squirrel	|	1
Bird	₭₭₭	5

How many squirrels are in the tree?

How many birds are in the tree?

This chart shows how many apples are in the basket.

Apples		Tally	Total
Red		⫽⫽⫽ ⫽⫽⫽	
Yellow		⫽⫽⫽ ⫽⫽	

What is the total number of red apples?

What is the total number of yellow apples?

Turn the page to learn about more things to tally.

Turn the page.

What are living things?

How do you think a bee, a flower, and a frog are alike?

Plants and animals are **living things**. Living things can grow and change. This flower grew from a seed.

Some living things move on their own. This frog can jump. Living things can be parents. Find the picture of the parent.

Nonliving things cannot move on their own. They cannot grow. Find the pictures of nonliving things.

Tally living and nonliving things.

Materials

 paper pencil

Process Skills

- observing
- classifying

Steps

1. Make a chart like the one in the picture.

2. Observe things around you.

3. Classify the things as living or nonliving.

4. Make a tally mark for each living and nonliving thing.

Share. Tell if you tallied more living or more nonliving things.

Lesson Review

1. Name three living things.

2. How can you tell that a rock is a nonliving thing?

3. **Draw** a living and a nonliving thing.

What is a habitat?

Tomatoes are growing in the garden. What other living things do you see?

A **habitat** is a place where plants and animals live. A habitat has everything a plant or animal needs.

This garden is a habitat for many living things. There is food, water, and air for the animals. There is sunlight, water, and air for the plants.

What animals live in this garden? What do they eat? Where do they find water?

Make a model of a garden habitat.

Materials

 tagboard　　crayons　　glue

craft stick　　scissors

Process Skills

- making and using models

Steps

1. Draw and cut out an animal picture.

2. Glue the picture to a craft stick.

3. Draw a garden that has plants, water, and animals.

4. Put your animal puppet in the **model** of the garden. Show it finding food and water.

Share. Name some other living things that might live in the garden.

Lesson Review

1. What is a habitat?

2. What living things might you find in a garden?

3. **Tell** what living things need.

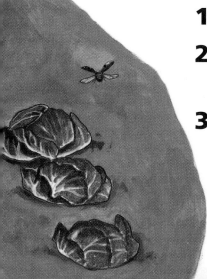

What lives in the ocean?

Did you ever wonder what lives in the ocean? You might be surprised!

Some animals have special body parts that help them live in the ocean.

The sea turtle has flippers that help it swim. The sea urchin has sharp spines that help protect it.

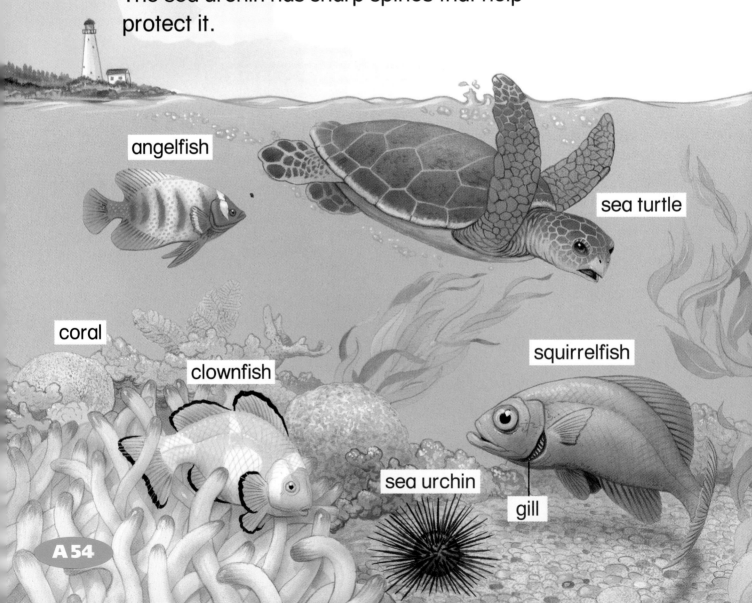

angelfish

sea turtle

coral

clownfish

squirrelfish

sea urchin

gill

Dolphins use a blowhole on top of their heads to breathe air. Fish use gills to breathe in the water. What other animals live in the ocean?

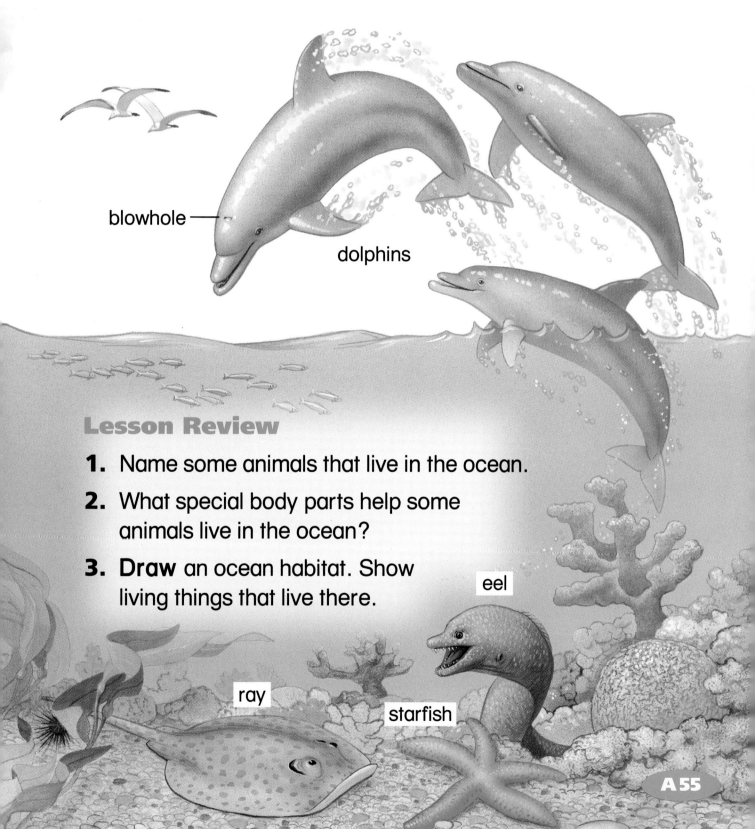

blowhole

dolphins

eel

ray

starfish

Lesson Review

1. Name some animals that live in the ocean.

2. What special body parts help some animals live in the ocean?

3. **Draw** an ocean habitat. Show living things that live there.

What lives in the forest and desert?

Pretend you are walking in a forest or a desert. What do you see and hear?

The forest is a habitat for living things. Trees grow in a forest. Animals use the trees in different ways. The squirrel makes a nest in the tree. The woodpecker finds insects under the bark. The newt lives in the shade of the trees.

The desert is a dry habitat. The kit fox, the elf owl, and the gila monster are some desert animals. Cactuses are desert plants that can live for a long time without water. You can find different kinds of cactuses in this picture.

Lesson Review

1. How do woodpeckers use trees?

2. What are some animals and plants that live in the desert?

3. **Write** about a trip you might take to a forest or desert.

How can you make a habitat?

Process Skills

Process Skills

- observing

Materials

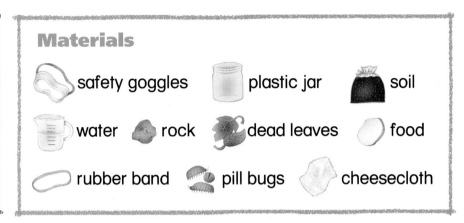

safety goggles · plastic jar · soil

water · rock · dead leaves · food

rubber band · pill bugs · cheesecloth

Steps

1. Put on your safety goggles.

2. Put soil in the jar. Add a little water.

3. Put a rock, dead leaves, sticks, and food in the jar.

4. Put pill bugs in the jar. Cover the jar.

5. Observe the pill bugs.

Think About Your Results

1. What did the pill bugs do after you put them in their new home?

2. What do pill bugs need in their home to stay alive?

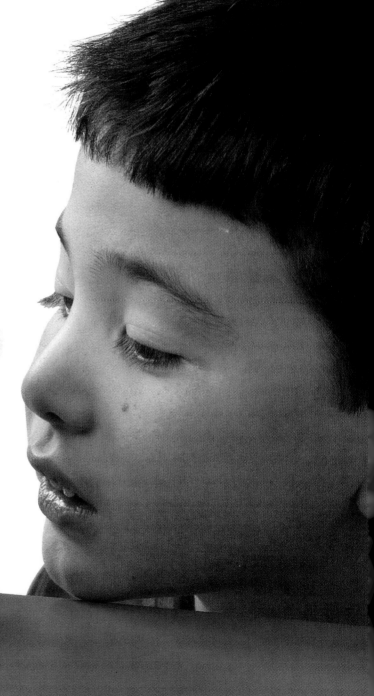 Inquire Further

Suppose you wanted to have more pill bugs. What changes would you make to the jar?

Chapter 3 Review

Reviewing Science Words

1. What can **living things** do?

2. How do you know that a book is a **nonliving thing**?

3. What might you find in a forest **habitat**?

Reviewing Science Ideas

1. Name a living and a nonliving thing.

2. Name a habitat. Tell what plants or animals might live there.

3. What are some things that an animal needs?

Make a model of a habitat.

Materials

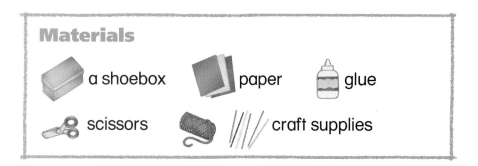

a shoebox   paper   glue

scissors   craft supplies

1. Choose a habitat.

2. Find out what living and nonliving things are in that habitat.

3. Make a model of the habitat. Show plants and animals. Show nonliving things.

4. Tell about the living and nonliving things in the habitat.

Unit A
Performance Review

You have learned many things about plants and animals. To celebrate what you know, you can have a party!

Plan your party.

1. Pick a project you will do for the party.

2. Decide what you will need.

3. Share your project with your friends.

Have a parade.

Choose an animal. Draw a picture of the animal and write its name on a sign. Use yarn to hang the sign around your neck. Have an animal parade. Try to make yourself look, move, and sound like your animal.

Play a game.

Write clues about a plant or animal. Read the clues. After each clue, give your partner a chance to guess the plant or animal.

Put on a puppet show.

Think of a story to tell about a plant or animal. Use a big box to make a puppet stage. Decorate it to look like a habitat for your plant or animal. Make puppets out of paper bags. Put on your show for the class.

Writing About Habitats

When you explain how things are alike and different, you are comparing. You can write sentences to compare and contrast things.

1. **Prewrite** Choose two habitats. Make a chart that tells about each habitat. List animals, plants, and nonliving things in your chart.

2. **Draft** Use the words in your chart to write sentences about each habitat. Tell how the habitats are alike and different.

3. **Revise** Read what you wrote. Do you like it?

4. **Edit** Check your writing to make sure it is correct. Make a neat copy.

5. **Publish** Share your chart and your writing with others. You can draw pictures of the habitats.

Unit B
Physical Science

Science and Technology
In Your World!

How does a blimp fly?

A blimp is a huge airship. A blimp floats in the sky because the gas inside is lighter than air. Blimps usually fly slowly and low. People flying in it get a good look at the earth.

Chapter 1
Grouping Objects

How can a vest help a firefighter?

This firefighter's special vest has sensors in it. When the air nearby gets too hot, the sensors tell a tiny computer. Then the vest sounds an alarm.

Chapter 2
Sound, Light, and Heat

What is a water escalator?

It is a large tube filled with water. The water moves around and around. It takes riders to the top of the water slide.

Chapter 3
Moving and Working

Chapter 1
Grouping Objects

Make a Little List

 Sing to the tune of *This Old Man*.

Water and juice
Can be poured.
But can you name any more?
Sit right down and make a little list.
Ask your friends what you have missed.

Keys will sink.

Pencils will float.

What else will sink? What else will float?

Sit right down and make a little list.

Ask your friends what you have missed.

Here's a riddle just for you.

How many things can water do?

Sit right down and make a little list.

Ask your friends what you have missed.

How can you group objects?

It is round. It is green and orange. It is smooth. It can float on water. You can see it on this page. What is it?

An **object** is a thing you can see or touch. Tell about the objects in the picture. What colors and shapes do you see? Which objects might feel smooth? Which might feel heavy?

You can learn about objects by sorting them into groups. How could you group these objects?

Float and sink objects.

Materials

 large container water

   classroom objects

Process Skills

- predicting
- observing

Process Skills

Steps

1. Choose an object.

2. **Predict.** Will it sink or float?

3. Put the object in water. **Observe.** Does it sink or float?

4. Try some other objects.

Share. Why do you think some objects sink and others float?

Lesson Review

1. What objects do you see around you? List five.

2. Look at the objects in your desk. How could you group these objects?

3. **Draw** a picture of two objects that sink and two objects that float.

How are solids and liquids different?

Would you put a book in a fishbowl? How silly! Would you put orange juice in your desk? What a mess!

The book and the blocks are solids. **Solids** have their own shape. They do not change shape when they are moved from place to place.

Water and orange juice are liquids. **Liquids** can change shape. If you pour a liquid from a tall pitcher into a round bowl, what shape will it be?

Solids and liquids both take up space and have a certain size. Which of these pictures shows a solid? Which shows a liquid? How do you know?

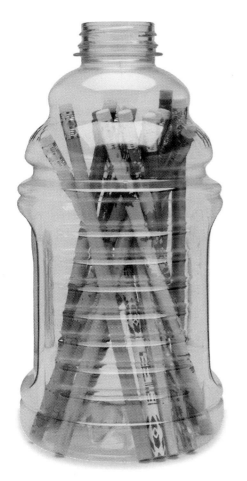 

Lesson Review

1. How can you tell if an object is a solid?

2. If you pour a liquid into a tall glass, what shape will it be?

3. **Draw** a solid and a liquid. Write an **S** under the solid. Write an **L** under the liquid.

What are gases like?

Suppose you pop a balloon. Can you see, hear, or feel what is inside?

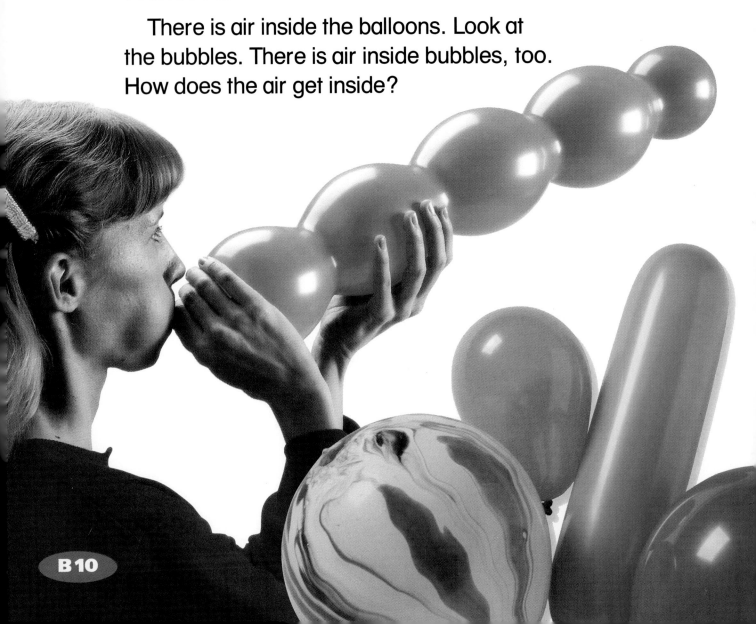

Gas takes up space. A gas has no shape of its own. It can change shape and size.

Air is made of gases. Air has no color. It has no taste. It is all around, but you cannot even see it!

There is air inside the balloons. Look at the bubbles. There is air inside bubbles, too. How does the air get inside?

Use objects to make bubbles.

Materials

 safety goggles   soapy water

 objects for making bubbles

- observing

Steps

1. Put on safety goggles.

2. Use different objects to make bubbles.

3. Observe the size and shape of the bubbles.

Share. Tell how bubbles made with different objects are alike and different.

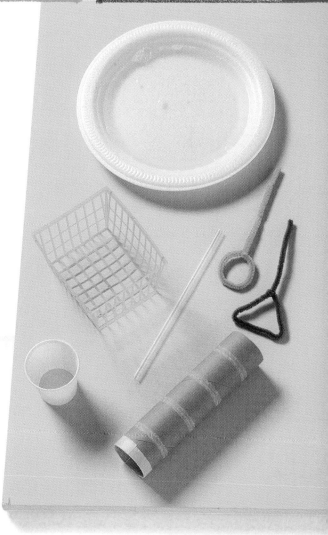

Lesson Review

1. Tell what a gas is like.

2. Where can you find air?

3. Draw an object you used to make bubbles. Draw the bubbles it made.

Predicting

When you predict, you tell what you think will happen. Look at the pictures. Predict what will happen next.

What might happen instead? Predict again.

What do you think is more likely to happen?

Look at the pictures. Predict what will happen next. Why do you think that will happen?

Turn the page to predict what will happen to bubbles.

Turn the page.

Experiment with bubbles.

Process Skills

Process Skills

- experimenting
- predicting

Materials

 safety goggles

2 plastic lids

 water with dish soap
water with hand soap

2 straws

Problem

Does hand soap or dish soap make bubbles that last longer?

Give Your Hypothesis

Will bubbles made with hand soap or dish soap last longer? Tell what you think.

Control the Variables

Make the bubbles the same size.

Test Your Hypothesis

Follow these steps to do the experiment.

1 Put on your safety goggles.

2 Work with a partner. Use hand soap and dish soap.

3 **Predict.** Will bubbles made with hand soap or dish soap last longer?

4 Spread a little soapy water on each lid.

5 Blow a bubble on one lid. At the same time, your partner blows a bubble on the other lid.

6 Which bubble lasted longer? Tally.

7 Do it ten times. Tally each time.

Collect Your Data

Use a chart like this one. Tally to show which bubble lasted longer.

Tally

hand soap	dish soap

Tell Your Conclusion

Compare your results and hypothesis. Which bubbles lasted longer?

 Inquire Further

What kind of soap makes bigger bubbles?

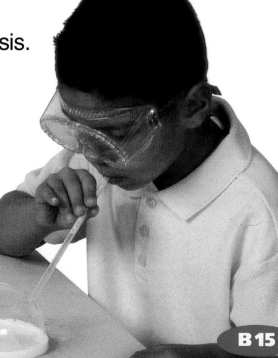

How can water change?

Put water into a freezer. Will you find water inside when you open the freezer the next day?

You know that water is a liquid. Water can change to a solid. This solid is called ice. Water changes to ice when it is so cold that it freezes. When the ice is heated, it changes back into a liquid. Look at the picture. Name the solid and the liquid.

before school   after school

Water can also change into a gas. When water changes to a gas, it **evaporates**. It goes into the air. You cannot see it.

Look at the pictures. What happened to the water in the puddle? It evaporated.

Lesson Review

1. What happens to water when it is very cold?

2. What happens to ice when it is heated?

3. **Tell** where water goes when it evaporates.

What happens when water evaporates?

Process Skills

- observing
- predicting

Materials

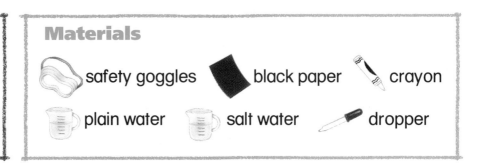

safety goggles   black paper   crayon

plain water   salt water   dropper

Steps

1. Put on your safety goggles.

2. Use a crayon to label one half of the paper **P** for plain water. Label the other half **S** for salt water.

3. Put a few drops of plain water on the **P** side.

4. Put a few drops of salt water on the **S** side.

5. **Observe.** Draw what you see.

6. **Predict.** Tell a friend what you think will happen the next day.

7. The next day, **observe** and draw what you see.

Think About the Results

1. What did you observe on the second day?

2. What happened to the water?

Inquire Further

What would happen if you used sugar water?

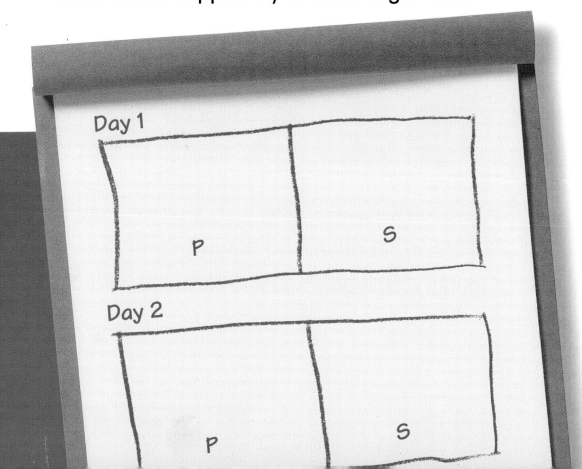

Chapter 1 Review

Reviewing Science Words

1. List three **objects** in your desk.

2. Find a picture of a **solid** , a **liquid** , and a **gas** .

3. Where can you find **air** ?

4. Where does water go when it **evaporates** ?

Reviewing Science Ideas

1. Put these objects into groups.
   Name each group.

2. How are solids and liquids different?

3. What happens to ice when it is heated?

4. What goes into a balloon when you blow it up?

Write a recipe for a drink.

Materials

paper   crayons   pencil

1. Choose a solid for your drink.
2. Choose a liquid for your drink.
3. Write a recipe that tells what to do with the solid and liquid.
4. Tell what might happen if your drink gets too cold or too hot.
5. Name your drink.

Chapter 2
Sound, Light, and Heat

Dark, Cool, and Quiet

♪ Sing to the tune of *Cockles and Mussels.*

The room that you stand in
is dark, cool, and quiet.
You want a big change
so now what can you do?

You open the shades.
Let the sun pour in brightly.
Then let in the puppy
who barks at your shoe.

Original lyrics by Gerri Brioso and Richard Freitas.
Produced by Children's Television Workshop.
Copyright © 1999 Sesame Street, Inc.

You might feel a bit silly,
the room is still chilly.
So drink some hot cocoa
and you'll warm up fast.

Things are much different,
More light, heat, and sounds.
It's brighter! It's louder!
You've warmed up at last!

What kinds of sounds are there?

A fire truck rushes down the street. A dog barks at cars. What a noisy corner!

Some sounds are loud. Loud sounds can warn you of danger. The siren on a fire truck warns people to get out of the way. What loud sounds have you heard?

Some sounds are soft. A whisper is a soft sound. What is the softest sound you can make?

If you were on this corner, what loud and soft sounds might you hear?

Make a drum.

Materials

safety goggles   small container

balloon   scissors   pencil

Steps

1. Put on your safety goggles.

2. Cut the end off of a balloon.

3. Stretch the balloon over the container.

4. Use a pencil to beat the drum.

5. **Observe** the sounds. Make loud sounds. Make soft sounds.

Share. Tell how you made loud and soft sounds.

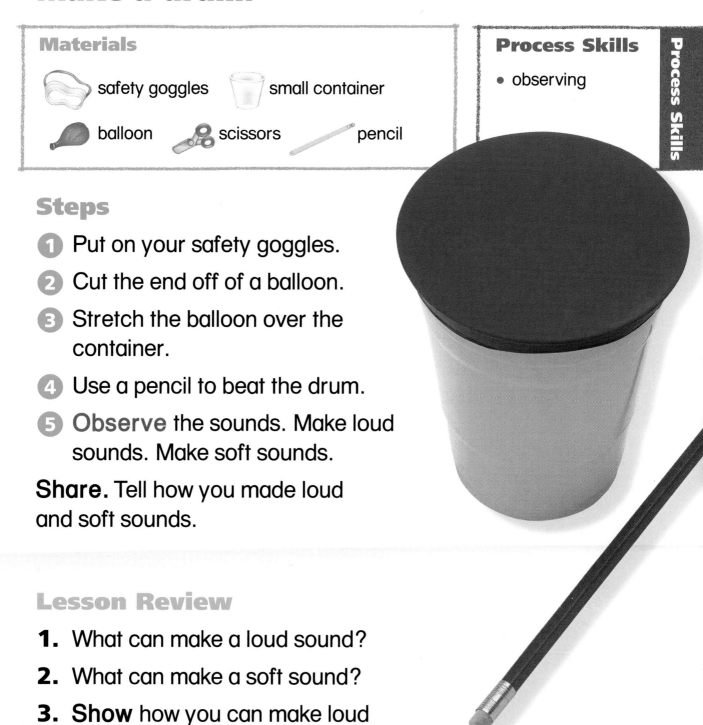

Lesson Review

1. What can make a loud sound?

2. What can make a soft sound?

3. **Show** how you can make loud and soft sounds with your drum.

How are sounds made?

Quietly hum your favorite song. Listen to the tune. How do the sounds change?

Some sounds are high. This triangle makes a high sound. Some sounds are low. This drum makes a low sound. When you sing or play a keyboard, you can make high and low sounds.

All sounds are made when something vibrates. **Vibrate** means to move back and forth very fast. When you beat a drum, parts of the drum vibrate to make sound.

Use a ruler to make sounds.

Materials

 safety goggles   ruler

Process Skills

- observing

Steps

1. Put on your safety goggles.

2. Hold one end of the ruler on your desk.

3. Snap the other end of the ruler.

4. **Observe.** What do you hear? What do you see?

Share. Tell what you heard and saw when you snapped the ruler.

Lesson Review

1. What happens when something vibrates?

2. Name something that can make a high sound and something that can make a low sound.

3. **Show** how a ruler vibrates to make sound.

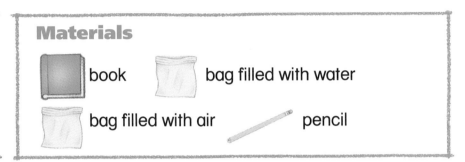

Does sound travel through things?

Process Skills

- observing

Materials

book   bag filled with water

bag filled with air   pencil

Steps

1 Put the book on a table. Put one ear on the book. Put your hand over your other ear.

2 Have your partner tap the pencil on the table. **Observe** what you hear.

3 Do it again with the bag of water and a bag with air inside.

4 Use a chart like the one in the picture. Write how well you hear the tapping sound.

Think About Your Results

1. When was the tapping sound loudest?

2. When was the tapping sound softest?

Inquire Further

Suppose you were trying to hear footsteps. Would you put your ear next to the ground or hold your head up in the air?

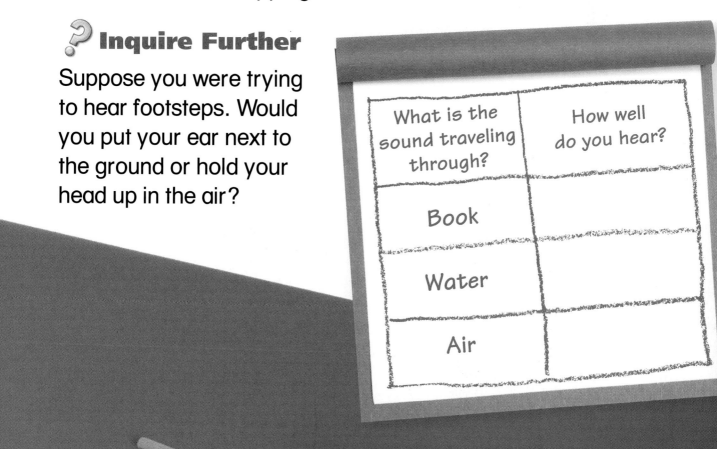

What is the sound traveling through?	How well do you hear?
Book	
Water	
Air	

How is a shadow made?

Think of a time when you saw a shadow. What shape did it have? What made the shadow?

Light comes from the sun, fire, or a light bulb. A shadow is made when something blocks the light. Light cannot go through this toy boat. The toy blocks the light and makes a **shadow**. Observe how the shape of the shadow is like the shape of the toy.

You can see shadows outside on a sunny day. What do you think is making the shadow in the picture below?

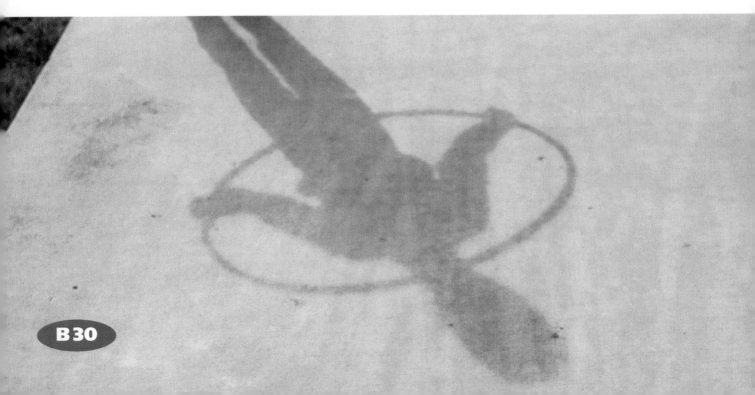

Observe shadows.

Materials

 pencil paper

Process Skills

- observing
- communicating (write)

Steps

1. Use a chart like this one.
2. **Observe** some shadows.
3. Draw the shadow.
4. **Write** what object made the shadow.

Share. Tell about one of the shadows you found.

Lesson Review

1. Where does light come from?
2. How is a shadow made?
3. **Draw** a picture of a shadow.

Telling Time

A clock has numbers and hands. The long hand is called the minute hand. It is pointing to 12.

The short hand is called the hour hand. It is pointing to 9. It is 9 o'clock.

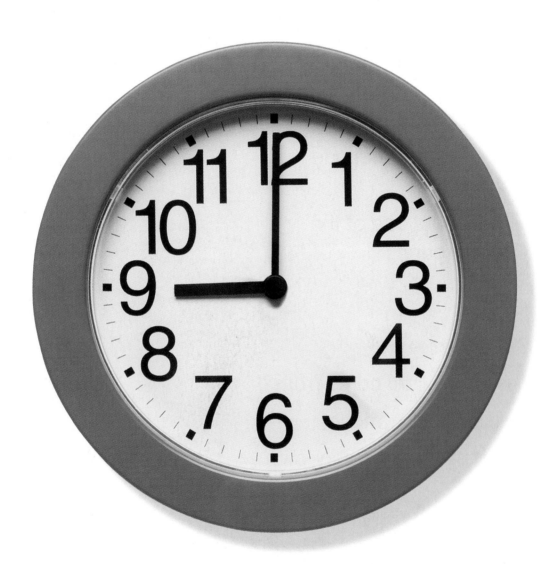

What time is it? What is happening at each time?

Turn the page for an activity about time and shadows.

Turn the page.

How do shadows change?

Process Skills

- observing

Materials

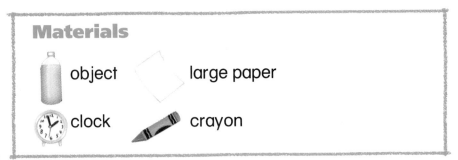

object

large paper

clock

crayon

Steps

1. Start this activity in the morning.

2. Choose an object.

3. Find a sunny place.

4. Put your object on the paper. Trace its shadow.

5 Write what time it is.

6 Do it again near lunchtime. Observe how the shadow has changed.

7 Do it again before going home. Observe again.

Think About Your Results

1. When was the shadow the longest?

2. When was the shadow the shortest?

? Inquire Further

How does the shadow under a tree change during the day?

What gives off heat?

On a hot summer day, would you like to play in the sun or in the shade of a tree?

Heat comes from the light of the sun. The sun shines on the land and water. It can also shine on you! When you are outside, you may feel warmer in a sunny place than in the shade.

Fire gives off heat. This picture shows a fire cooking marshmallows.

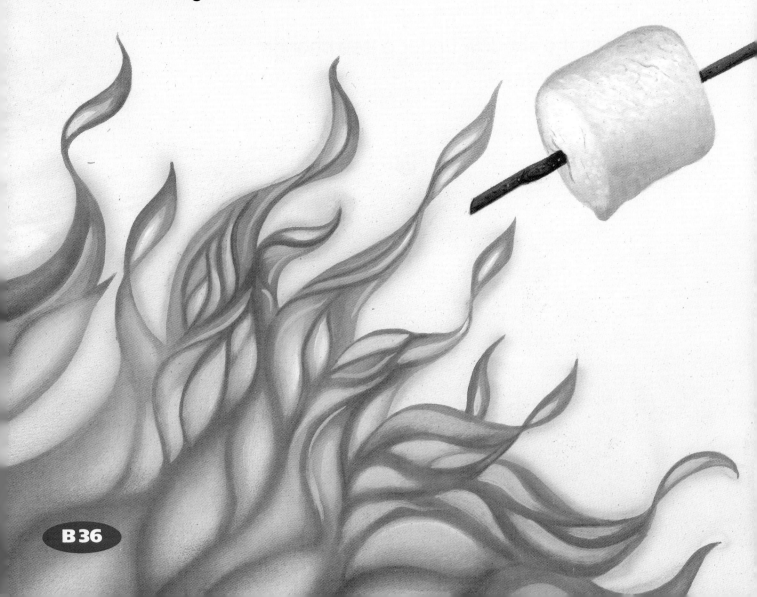

Heat comes from other things too. Rubbing things together can give off heat. Lamps, stoves, and toasters give off heat. What else do you know about that gives off heat?

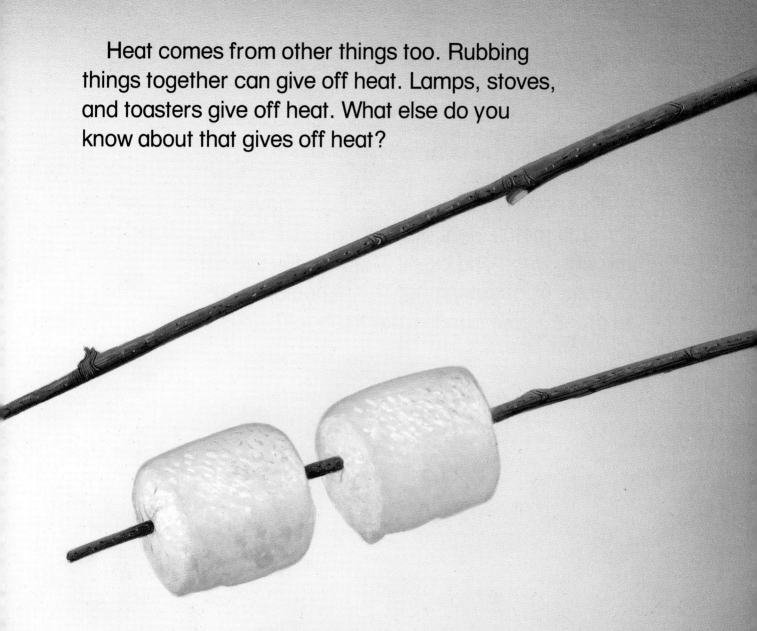

Lesson Review

1. What comes from the light of the sun?

2. What can you feel when you rub your hands together?

3. **Draw** three things that give off heat.

What feels hot?

Mmm! Here is some hot cocoa to drink! Be careful, the pan is very hot!

This pan is made of metal. Heat moves easily through metal. Heat does not move easily through wood and cloth. The wood keeps the counter from getting hot. What could you use to protect your hands from the heat?

If you put hot cocoa in this metal cup it would feel hot. This foam cup does not feel hot. Heat does not move easily through foam.

Lesson Review

1. Name something that heat moves through easily.

2. Name something that heat does not move through easily.

3. Would you put a hot drink in a metal cup or a foam cup? Why?

How can you keep an ice cube frozen?

Process Skills

- observing

Materials

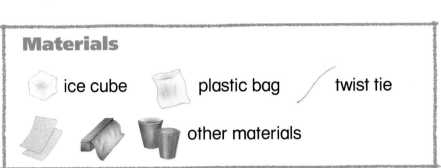

ice cube   plastic bag   twist tie

other materials

Steps

1. Gather materials.

2. Use the materials to make a container that keeps an ice cube frozen.

3. Put the ice cube in a plastic bag. Put it in your container.

4 When your teacher tells you, take the plastic bag out of the container. **Observe.** How much ice is still frozen?

5 Compare your ice cube with others in your class.

Think About Your Results

1. Which containers kept ice frozen longer?

2. Why do you think ice stayed frozen longer in some containers than in others?

? Inquire Further

How could you change your container to keep ice frozen longer?

Chapter 2 Review

Reviewing Science Words

1. What can **vibrate** to make sound?

2. Tell how you could make a **shadow**.

Reviewing Science Ideas

1. What loud and soft sounds have you heard?

2. What happens when something vibrates?

3. How does a shadow change during the day?

4. Name three things that give off heat.

5. Why is a foam cup sometimes used for hot cocoa?

Tell a story.

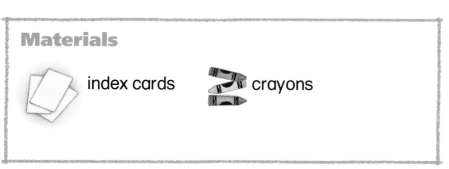
1 Use 3 cards. Draw a picture that shows sound, a picture that shows light or a shadow, and a picture that shows heat.

2 Put each picture into the class pile of sound, light, or heat cards.

3 Choose a card from each pile.

4 Tell a story that uses 2 of the 3 cards.

Chapter 3

Moving and Working

On the Move

♪ Sing to the tune of *Turkey in the Straw.*

If you want to move a ball
from here to over there,

You can kick it with your foot
and send it through the air.

If the ball's too heavy,
don't you despair.

Make a ramp, send it rolling.
It will get over there.

Push it or pull it.
Move it everywhere.

Roll it down, throw it up,
high into the air.

What else can you do
to make things move?

Try a magnet or a lever
and your moving will improve.

Original lyrics by Gerri Brioso and Richard Freitas.
Produced by Children's Television Workshop.

How can you move things?

It is fun to ride in a wagon. How are these children making the wagon move?

You can **push** or **pull** to make things move. The girl holding the handle is pulling the wagon. Her sister is pushing from behind.

When you put clothes away, you pull to open a drawer. To close the drawer, you push it shut. What else can you pull or push?

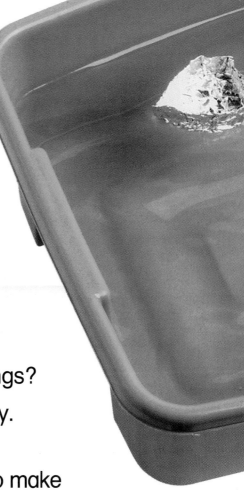
Push and pull a boat.

Materials

 aluminum foil   bowl of water

Process Skills

• making and
  using models
• classifying

Process Skills

Steps

1. Use foil to **make a model** of a boat.

2. Set the boat on the water.

3. Find ways to make the boat move.

4. **Classify** the ways. Each time you make the boat move, tell if you are using a push or a pull.

Share. Show two ways you can move your boat.

Lesson Review

1. What are two ways you can move things?

2. Tell about something you moved today. Did you push or pull?

3. **Tell** how you used a push and a pull to make your boat move.

Using a Map

A map shows how to get from place to place.
This map shows how to get from a home to
the park.

How can the car get from the blue house to the school? Use your finger to show how the car can go.

Turn the page to learn more about how things move.

Turn the page.

What ways do things move?

Would you rather bounce a ball or toss a bean bag? Would you rather twirl a *jump rope* or spin a top?

You can make things move in many ways. You can throw a ball up and watch it fall back to the ground. You can roll a ball far. You can tap it so it hardly moves.

Find the two marbles in this picture. Tell about how they move. What might make them go fast, slow, or change direction?

Make a maze.

Materials

 blocks ⬤ table tennis ball

╱ straw

Steps

1 Build a maze.

2 Put the ball at one end of the maze.

3 Blow the ball with the straw. Observe how the ball moves, stops, and changes direction.

4 Move the ball through the maze. Then move it back again.

Share. Draw a map of your maze. Draw a line to show where the ball went.

Lesson Review

1. Name different ways that you can make things move.

2. What can make a marble go fast?

3. Tell how you changed the direction of the ball.

What does a magnet attract?

Some are round. Some are fancy. One is shaped like a horseshoe. Where have you seen magnets?

This picture shows many kinds of **magnets**. A magnet pulls some things toward it. It **attracts** these things. How can you find out what a magnet attracts?

A magnet can **repel** another magnet. When a magnet repels another magnet, it pushes it away.

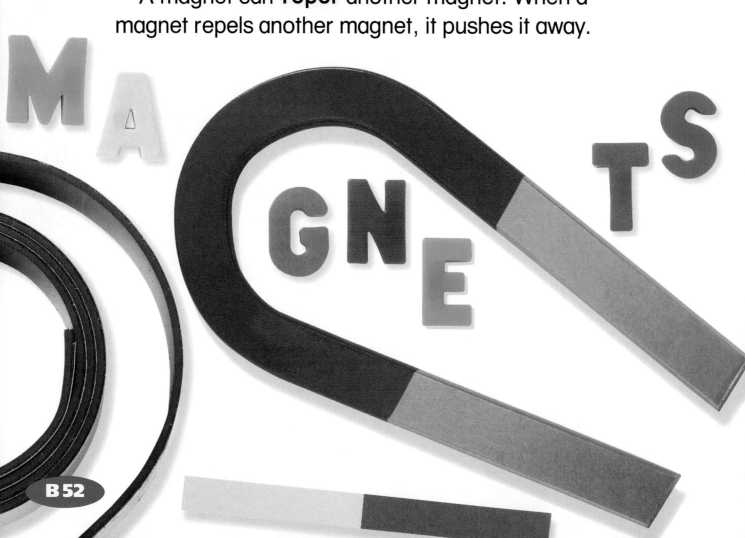

Find out what a magnet attracts.

Materials

 magnet paper

   classroom objects

Process Skills

- classifying

Steps

1. Write **attracts** on one paper.
   Write **does not attract** on the other paper.

2. Test things with a magnet.

3. **Classify** the things. Put them on the correct paper.

Share. Tell what other things you would like to test with the magnet.

Lesson Review

1. What can a magnet attract?

2. List three things that are not attracted to a magnet.

3. **Tell** what you observed about things that the magnet attracted.

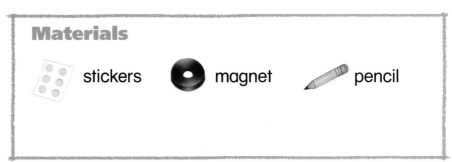

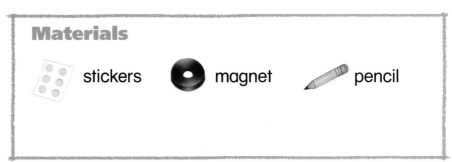

Investigate Activity

Can magnets push and pull?

Process Skills	Materials
• observing	stickers magnet pencil

Steps

1 Put a sticker on each side of a magnet. Draw a car on each sticker.

2 Use your car to pull your partner's car. **Observe.**

3 Use your car to push your partner's car. **Observe.** When your car pushes, it must not touch your partner's car.

4 Use a map like the one shown. Push your partner's car along the road to the store.

5 Pull your partner's car back to the garage.

Think About Your Results

1. Tell how you pulled your partner's car.

2. Tell how you pushed your partner's car.

Inquire Further

What else can your car pull along the road?

How do people use machines?

A tractor and a car are both machines. Did you know that a hammer and a can opener are machines, too?

These workers use some kinds of **simple machines** to build a house. Simple machines make work easier.

A **wheel** helps to move a heavy load.

A **ramp** makes it easier to move things up or down.

A **pulley** is used to lift a big box.

A **lever** can be used to take a lid off a box.

Lesson Review

1. What do simple machines do?

2. How could you use a ramp?

3. **Draw** a machine you use that has a wheel.

How does a lever work?

Process Skills

- observing

Materials

pencil   book   wooden ruler

Steps

1. Set up a book, pencil, and ruler as shown in the picture. The pencil is under the 20 centimeter mark. The book is on the 5.

2. Push down on the end of the ruler to lift the book.

3. Do it again with the pencil under the 15.

4. Do it again with the pencil under the 10.

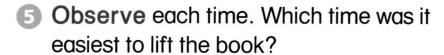

5 **Observe** each time. Which time was it easiest to lift the book?

6 Draw a picture of the ruler, book, and pencil. Show where the pencil is when it is easiest to lift the book.

Think About Your Results

1. Was it easiest to lift the book with the pencil under the 10, 15, or 20?

2. Would it be easier to lift the book with the pencil under the 12 or 18 centimeter mark?

Inquire Further

A ruler makes a good lever. What else could you as a lever?

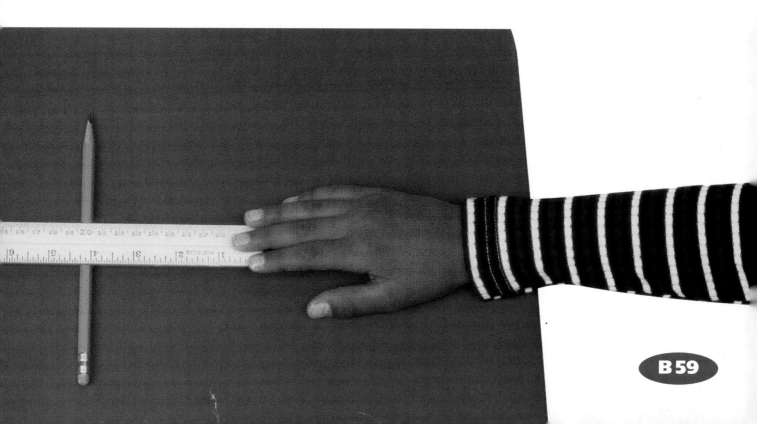

Chapter 3 Review

Reviewing Science Words

1. Name something that you can **push**.

2. Name something that you can **pull**.

3. What can a **magnet** do?

4. Name something that a magnet can **attract**.

5. What happens when a magnet **repels**?

6. Match the picture of each **simple machine** to the word.

ramp

pulley

lever

wheel

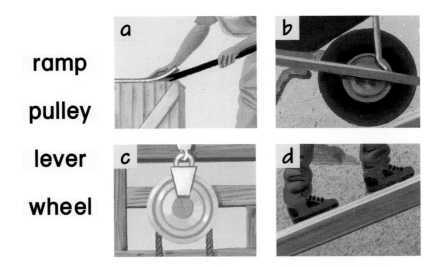

Reviewing Science Ideas

1. How can you change the way a ball moves?

2. What can you do with a lever?

Design a toy.

1. Make a poster of your toy.

2. Name your toy.

3. Label the parts.

4. Tell how to use your toy. Use science words such as push, pull, wheel, lever, ramp, pulley, and magnet.

Unit B
Performance Review

There are solids, liquids, and gases all around you. There is sound, light, and heat. People are moving and working. Show what you know about all these things in a class museum.

Plan a museum.

1. Choose a project to do.

2. Think about what you need to make your project.

3. What will you do first?

Make an exhibit.

Label one side of your exhibit **push** and the other side **pull**. Look for objects that you move by pushing or pulling. Put the objects in the exhibit. Tell how you push or pull to make them move.

Tape record sounds.

Think of different ways to make sounds. Record the sounds on a tape recorder. Play your recording. Have your friends tell about the sounds and guess how you made them.

Tell a story.

Think of a solid, a liquid, and a gas. Tell a story. The solid, liquid, and gas should be part of your story. When you tell the story, let the class listen for the solid, liquid, and gas.

Writing Clues to Describe an Object

You can describe something without telling what it is. When *you* do this, you give a clue about it. You can describe how it looks, sounds, feels, smells, or tastes. You can tell what it is *made* of or what it is used for.

1. **Prewrite** Choose an object. Observe the object. Think of clues to describe it.

2. **Draft** Write clues that describe the object.

3. **Revise** Read the clues. Will others be able to guess the object? Make changes if you want to.

4. **Edit** Check your writing to make sure it is correct. Make a neat copy.

5. **Publish** Share your clues with others. See if they can guess the object.

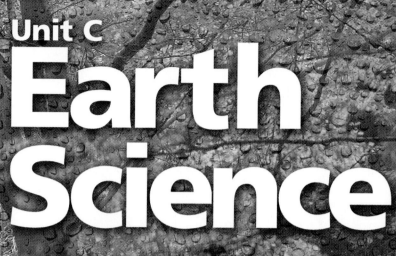

Unit C
Earth Science

Science and Technology
In Your World!

How can an old tire help a cow?

This cow is standing on a special mat made from recycled tires. The cow can rest on the mat and be comfortable.

Chapter 1
The Earth

What is the weather like?

Is it cold in Canada? Is it sunny in Spain? Find out what the weather is like around the world. Use the Internet.

Chapter 2
Weather

Back Forward Reload Home Search Guides Images Print Security Stop

Locations http://www.weather_on_net.com

Welcome to WWW Weather Foreca

Weather Maps

Forecast

Storm Prediction

Warnings

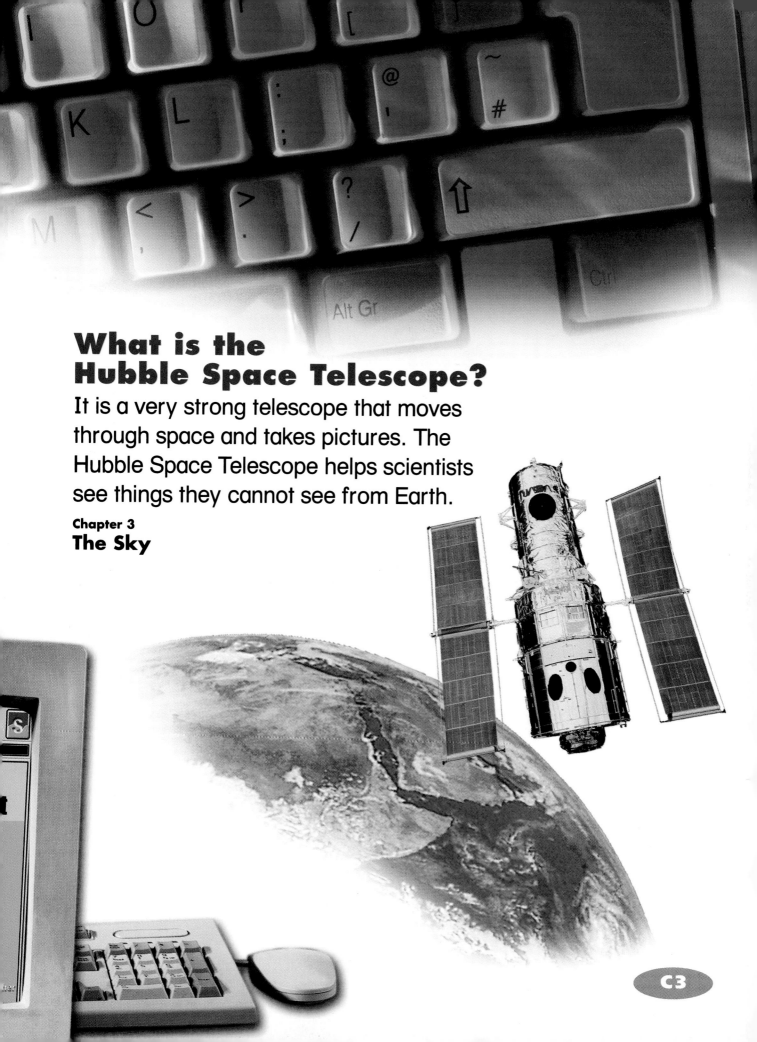

What is the Hubble Space Telescope?

It is a very strong telescope that moves through space and takes pictures. The Hubble Space Telescope helps scientists see things they cannot see from Earth.

Chapter 3
The Sky

Chapter 1
The Earth

On Top of a Mountain

 Sing to the tune of *On Top of Old Smokey.*

Climb up on a mountain
Sit under a tree
And look at Earth's wonders.
So many to see.

You'll see rocks and soil
As you look here and there.
All sizes and colors.
It's fun to compare.

There's clear sparkling water
In rivers and lakes.
With fresh air for breathing
A fine home Earth makes.

Using a Bar Graph

A bar graph helps you compare groups.
This bar graph shows what colors children like.

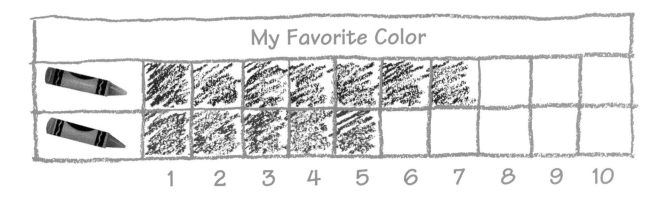

This bar graph shows that 5 children like
blue. It shows that 7 children like red. Do more
children like blue or red?

What does this bar graph show?

Snacks We Like

| | 1 | 2 | 3 | 4 | 5 | 6 | 7 | 8 | 9 | 10 |

How many carrots are there?

How many pretzels are there?

How many orange slices are there?

How many more pretzels are there than carrots?

Turn the page for an activity that uses bar graphs.

Turn the page.

C7

What are rocks like?

Looking for rocks is fun. You can find them in dirt and in water. Some houses and roads are made of rocks. Rocks are everywhere!

Rocks come in many sizes, colors, and shapes. Rocks can be shiny or dull. They can be rough or smooth.

Air, water, and ice can change rocks. This is called **weathering**. Rough rocks can become smooth. Big rocks can break into smaller pieces. Tiny bits of sand were once parts of rocks!

Graph rocks.

Materials

 rocks

Process Skills

- observing
- classifying

Steps

1 Observe the rocks. How are they alike and different?

2 Use a graph like this one. Classify the rocks into two groups

3 Label the graph.

Share. Tell about your graph.

Lesson Review

1. What words can you use to tell about rocks?

2. How can weathering change rocks?

3. Show another way to sort and graph the rocks.

Experiment with weathering.

Process Skills

Process Skills

- experimenting
- observing

Materials

 chalk

 2 containers with lids

 clock

Problem

How can weathering change chalk?

Give Your Hypothesis

If you shake chalk, will it weather?
Tell what you think.

C10

Control the Variables

Put chalk into each container. You will shake one container. You will not shake the other.

Test Your Hypothesis

Follow these steps to do the **experiment**.

1. **Observe** the pieces of chalk. Draw how they look.

2. Put chalk into each container. Put on the lids.

3. Shake one container for one minute.

4. Open the containers and **observe** the pieces of chalk again. Draw how they look now.

Collect Your Data

Use a chart like this to draw the chalk.

Tell Your Conclusion

Compare the results to your hypothesis. How did the chalk change?

 Inquire Further

What will happen if you put water and chalk in the container?

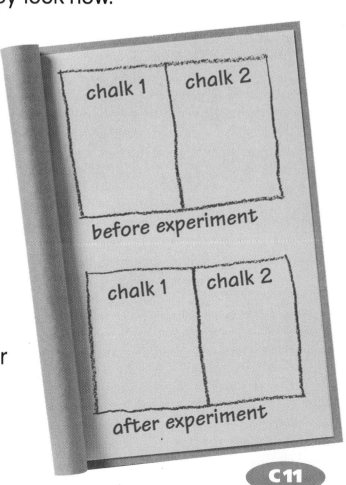

What is soil?

Did you ever dig a hole in the ground? What did you see?

   Soil is made of tiny bits of rock. Some soil also has clay, sand, or parts of living things that have died.

   Living things use soil in many ways. Some animals find food in the soil. Others live under the ground.

People use soil to grow food. Roots of plants and trees grow in soil. What can you see in this picture of soil?

Lesson Review

1. What is soil made of?

2. How do living things use soil?

3. **Draw** some soil. Show what you might find in the soil.

What kinds of soils are there?

Process Skills

• observing

Materials

safety goggles

3 paper plates

craft sticks

hand lens

3 kinds of soil

Steps

1 Put on your safety goggles.

2 Number the plates 1, 2, and 3.

3 Put a different soil on each plate.

4 **Observe** each soil.

5 Draw what you **observe**.
Use a chart like this one.

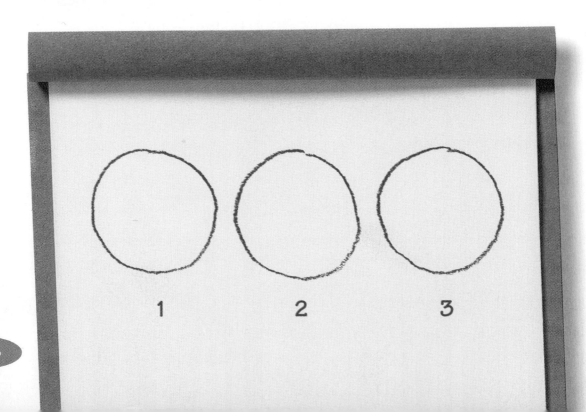

1   2   3

Think About Your Results

1. Tell how the soils are alike or different.

2. What did you find in the soils?

 Inquire Further

In which soil would seeds grow the fastest?

What is the earth like?

Choose a hill or a desert, a lake or a mountain. Where would you like to go on the earth?

The earth has air all around it. The earth has land and water. Look at the land and water in these pictures. In some places, the land is flat. In other places, there are mountains. What is the land like where you live?

Most of the water on the earth is in the oceans. There is water in rivers, streams, and lakes too. Do you live near water?

The globe shows the shape of the earth. It is shaped like a ball. The blue places on the globe show water. The rest is land. Do you see more water or land on the globe?

Lesson Review

1. What is all around the earth?

2. What is the shape of the earth?

3. **Show** where there is water and land on the globe.

How do people use air, land, and water?

Living things need air to stay alive. Plants need air to grow. People need clean air to breathe. People have been working together to keep air clean.

People can keep the land clean too. The girl in this picture is throwing away trash. How can you help keep the land clean?

People need clean water to stay alive and healthy. People use water for drinking, cooking, and washing. How are people in the picture using water?

You can help keep water clean. You can try not to use more water than you need.

Lesson Review

1. How can you help keep the land clean?

2. Name three ways people use water.

3. **Draw** a picture that shows one way to use water.

What can you reuse and recycle?

Find the metal, plastic, glass, and paper in the picture. What can you do with these things?

When you **reuse** something, you use it again. Think before you throw away a box or a toy. Can you use the box in a different way? Could someone play with the toy?

Another way to use something again is to **recycle** . Plastic can be recycled. It can be melted and made into new things. Plastic bottles might become a new chair!

Reuse a container.

Materials

 container  art supplies

 scissors

Process Skills

- communicating (tell)

Steps

1. Think of a way to reuse your container.

2. Use art supplies to make your idea.

Share. Tell what you made.

Lesson Review

1. Name something you can reuse.

2. Name one thing that can be recycled.

3. **Tell** what would happen if people reused more things.

Chapter 1 Review

Reviewing Science Words

1. How can **weathering** change rocks?

2. What might you find in **soil**?

3. Tell how you could **reuse** a shoe box.

4. What are some things you can **recycle**?

Reviewing Science Ideas

1. What words can you use to tell about rocks?

2. How can rocks change?

3. Where is there water on the earth?

4. What are some ways people use water?

Make an earth book.

Materials

paper   art supplies

1 Make a round book.

2 Draw the earth on the cover.

3 Draw or write one thing about the earth on each page.

4 Share your book. Read the words. Show the pictures.

Chapter 2
Weather

The Weather Changed

🎵 Sing to the tune of *Bingo*.

The weather changed from yesterday,

And will it change tomorrow?

Will there be sun or rain?

Will the wind blow or not?

Will it be hot or cold?

We'll only know tomorrow.

The weather changes month to month,
And also with the seasons.
Which season's very cold?
Which season's very warm?
Which season makes leaves fall?
What is your favorite season?

Original lyrics by Gerri Brioso and Richard Freitas.
Produced by Children's Television Workshop.

Using a Chart

You can use a chart to find information. A chart has columns and rows. Columns go up and down. Rows go across.

Weather

Day	Weather	Temperature
Monday	☁	hot
Tuesday	○	warm
Wednesday	🌧	cool

This chart tells about the weather. Point to the first column. This column tells the name of the day.

Point to the second and third columns. What do these columns tell about?

Our Favorite Weather

Name	Weather	Temperature
Tom		cold
Anna		warm
Lee		hot

What does this chart tell about?

What does each column show?

What is Tom's favorite weather?

What is Anna's favorite temperature?

Turn the page to learn more about using a chart.

Turn the page.

What can you tell about weather?

Look out a window. What is it like outside? Do you need a raincoat and an umbrella?

It might be sunny, cloudy, or rainy. It might be still or windy. All of these words tell about the weather. **Temperature** is how hot or cold it is. What is the temperature outside today?

Weather is always changing. Think of what the weather was like yesterday. Is the weather different today?

Chart the weather.

Materials

 paper  crayons

Process Skills

- observing

Steps

1 **Observe** the weather.

2 Use a chart like this one. Draw a sun, rain, snow, or clouds to show the weather.

3 Tell about the temperature.

4 Do this for 5 days.

Share. Tell how the weather changed this week.

Weather Chart

Day	Weather	Temperature
Monday		cool
Tuesday		
Wednesday		
Thursday		
Friday		

Lesson Review

1. What words can you use to tell about the temperature?

2. Tell what the weather is like today.

3. **Draw** a picture of yourself in your favorite kind of weather.

How can you observe wind?

Process Skills

- observing

Materials

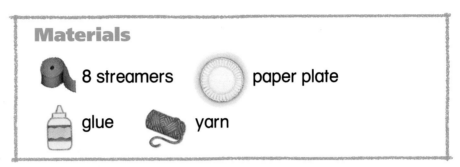

8 streamers   paper plate

glue   yarn

Steps

1. Turn the paper plate upside down. Glue streamers to the plate.

2. Tie yarn through holes in the plate.

3. Blow gently on the streamers. **Observe** and draw the results.

4. Now blow hard on the streamers. **Observe** and draw the results.

5 Go outside. **Observe** and draw the streamers blowing in the wind.

Think About Your Results

1. What happened when you blew gently on the streamers?

2. What happened when you blew hard on the streamers?

Inquire Further

What kinds of things might happen on a very windy day?

How can you measure temperature?

On a hot day, you can wear shorts outside. If it is cold, you might need a coat. How do you know how hot or cold it is?

A **thermometer** measures the temperature. The red line in a thermometer shows how hot or cold it is.

It is a hot day. The red line in this thermometer is high.

It is a cold day. The red line in this thermometer is low.

Use a thermometer.

Materials

 thermometer   cup of cold water

Process Skills

- observing
- estimating and measuring

Steps

1 **Observe** the red line in your thermometer.

2 Put your thumb over the round end of the thermometer. **Observe** what happens to the red line.

3 Put the thermometer in cold water.

4 **Observe** the red line again.

Share. Tell which time the thermometer **measured** the lowest temperature.

Lesson Review

1. What does a thermometer tell about the weather?

2. Tell where the red line in a thermometer might be on a hot day.

3. **Tell** what happened to the red line when you put the thermometer in cold water.

How do clouds form?

Are there clouds in the sky today? What do they look like? How did they get there?

There is water in the air. You cannot see it. It is called **water vapor** . When the air cools, the water vapor in it forms clouds.

Clouds are made of tiny drops of water or ice. The water or ice can fall from clouds as rain, snow, or hail.

Fog is a cloud that is near the ground. It is hard to see through fog. ▼

▲ These white, puffy clouds look like cotton balls.

You might see a cloud
like this before a storm. ▼

▲ These wispy clouds are
very high in the sky.

Lesson Review

1. What is water vapor?

2. What are clouds made of?

3. **Draw** a cloud. Tell what you know about the
kind of cloud you drew.

How can you make a cloud?

Process Skills

- observing

Materials

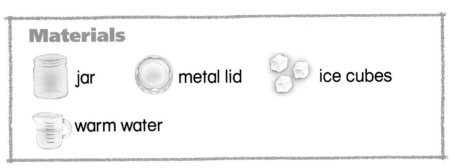

jar   metal lid   ice cubes

warm water

Steps

1 Rinse the jar in warm water.

2 Put a little warm water in the jar.

3 Place the lid upside down on top of the jar.

4 Put ice cubes on the lid.

5 **Observe** what happens inside the jar.

Think About Your Results

1. What happened inside the jar?

2. Draw what happened.

 Inquire Further

What would happen
if you did not put ice
on the lid?

How can you stay safe in bad weather?

A storm is coming! You need to stay safe. What should you do?

Stormy weather can be dangerous. Strong wind and heavy rain can harm houses and cause floods. During bad weather, listen to a weather report. The report will tell your family how to stay safe.

During a lightning storm, stay away from trees. Go inside. ▼

▲ During a tornado, go to the safest part of your home. Stay away from windows.

▲ During a blizzard, stay inside and keep warm.

Lesson Review

1. Why should you listen to a weather report during a storm?

2. Where is a safe place to be during a lightning storm?

3. **Draw** a picture showing what you and your family might do during a storm.

What are seasons like?

Do you have a favorite time of the year?
What do you like about that time?

A **season** is a time of the year. The
seasons are winter, spring, summer, and fall.
The temperature changes from season to season.
What changes do you see in these pictures?

Winter

Spring

Summer

Fall

Dress for the seasons.

Materials

 crayons paper

Process Skills

- classifying

Steps

1. Choose a season.

2. Draw yourself doing an outdoor activity in that season. Show what clothes you would wear.

3. Work in a group. **Classify** your pictures as summer, fall, winter, and spring.

Share. Tell how the clothes you drew are right for the season.

Lesson Review

1. Name the four seasons.

2. What is the coldest season of the year?

3. **Tell** what you might do during each season.

What do animals do in winter?

Brrr! It is a cold winter day. You need a coat and hat to stay warm when you play outside.

Animals find ways to stay warm in winter too. Some animals **migrate**, or move to a warmer place. These geese are flying south where the winter is warmer. Whales, butterflies, and other animals also migrate.

Some animals **hibernate**, or have a long, deep sleep. Woodchucks hibernate all winter in a hole in the ground. In spring, they come out and look for food.

These pictures show the same arctic fox. In summer, the fox's fur is brown. In winter, the fur is white. White fur helps the fox hide in snow.

Lesson Review

1. Why do some animals migrate?

2. Tell about an animal that hibernates.

3. **Tell** how white fur helps the fox in winter.

Chapter 2 Review

Reviewing Science Words

1. What words can you use to tell about the **temperature**?

2. What does a **thermometer** tell you?

3. Where is **water vapor**?

4. List the four **seasons**.

5. Why do some animals **migrate**?

6. What do animals do when they **hibernate**?

Reviewing Science Ideas

1. What words can you use to tell about weather?

2. What are clouds made of?

3. What should you do when a storm is coming?

4. Tell what clothing you might wear in cold weather.

Today is cloudy and rainy.

Report the weather.

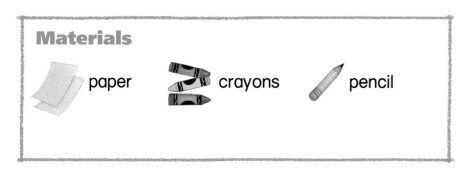
1 Write a weather report.

2 Use words to tell about the weather. Is it hot or cold? Is it sunny or rainy? What season is it?

3 Draw a picture that shows what to wear outside.

4 Tell what you think the weather will be like tomorrow.

Chapter 3
The Sky

Up in the Sky

♫ Sing to the tune of *Take Me Out to the Ballgame.*

In the sky is a bright light.

A light that we call the sun.

It gives us daylight and warmth and heat.

Play in the sun, it just cannot be beat!

But at night,

We can't see the sunshine.

We often can see the moon.

Did you know,

That,

Moonlight is sunlight,

That shines on the moon!

How are day and night different?

The sun is shining. It is time to get up.
A new day is beginning!

Earth is always turning. The sun shines on part of Earth. Where the sun shines, it is day. Where do you see the sun in the morning? Where do you see it at noon? Where do you see it in the evening?

Part of Earth is turned away from the sun. It is night on this part of Earth. It is dark. You might see stars or the moon. Sometimes you can see the moon during the day too!

Compare the day and night sky.

Materials

 crayons   construction paper

   art supplies

Process Skills

- observing

Process Skills

Steps

1. **Observe** the day sky.

2. Make a picture of the day sky.

3. Think about what you might **observe** in the night sky.

4. Make a picture of the night sky.

Share. Tell how the day and night sky are alike and different.

Lesson Review

1. How do you know when it is day?

2. How do you know when it is night?

3. **Tell** what you might see in the night sky and in the day sky.

Why do we need the sun?

Find the sun in the picture. Does it look bigger or smaller than the tractor?

The sun may look smaller than the tractor, but it is really very big. It is much, much bigger than Earth. The sun looks small because it is so far away.

Plants and animals need the sun. You need the sun. Almost all living things need the sun. Without the sun, there would be almost no life on Earth.

Find out why the sun looks small.

Materials

 ruler paper plate

Steps

1. **Measure** across a paper plate.

2. Have your partner hold the plate. Move 5 steps away from your partner.

3. Hold up the ruler in front of you. **Measure** how big the plate looks now.

Share. Tell how the size of the plate looked different.

Lesson Review

1. Why does the sun look small?

2. Name two living things that need the sun.

3. **Tell** how you can make the plate look smaller.

What is the moon like?

It is nighttime. Look up in the sky. You might see the *moon!*

A **telescope** can help you see things that are far away. This girl is using a telescope to look at the moon.

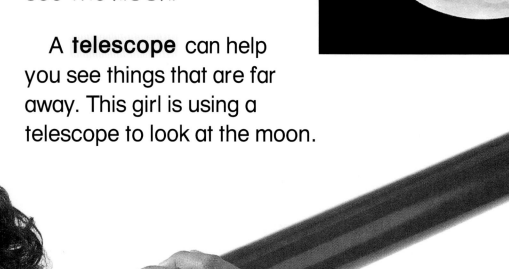

Look at the different shapes of the moon. The shapes of the moon are called **phases**. On some nights, the moon looks round. This is called a full moon. At other times, you see smaller parts of the moon. Sometimes, you cannot see the moon at all.

The moon does not make its own light. Light from the sun shines on the moon. You only see the part of the moon that has light shining on it.

Lesson Review

1. What does a telescope do?

2. What makes the moon look like it is shining?

3. **Draw** three phases of the moon.

Real and Imaginary

Some things are real. Some things are imaginary.

Which child is telling about something real? Which child is telling about something imaginary?

The clouds are white.

There is a rabbit in the sky.

Look at the pictures. Tell about the picture that shows something real. Tell about the picture that shows something imaginary.

Turn the page to learn about something real and something imaginary.

Turn the page.

What are stars like?

Guess how many stars are in the sky?
There are too many to count!

Stars are made of hot gases that glow. Stars give off their own light. Our sun is a star. It is the star closest to Earth.

Long ago, people imagined that lines connected groups of stars. The lines and stars looked like pictures in the night sky.

Big Dipper

Look at these pictures. Find a cup with a long handle. Look at the man. Find the stars that make his belt. What is the name of each group of stars?

Orion

Lesson Review

1. What is a star made of?

2. What star is closest to Earth?

3. **Draw** a picture of a group of stars. Write its name.

What star picture can you make?

Process Skills

- making and using models

Materials

construction paper   white crayon

dots   glue

Steps

1. Use dots to make a picture. The dots are a **model** of stars in the sky.

2. Glue the dots to the paper.

3. Use a crayon to connect the dots.

4. Give your star picture a name.

Think About Your Results

1. Are stars in the sky really joined together?

2. What star pictures have you seen in the night sky?

Inquire Further

What other star pictures can you make?

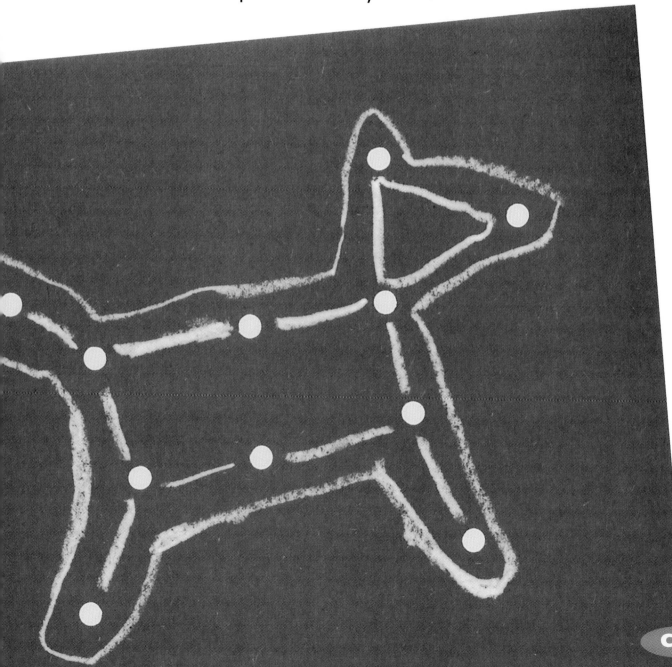

Chapter 3 Review

Reviewing Science Words

1. What can you use a **telescope** for?

2. Tell about one **phase** of the moon.

Reviewing Science Ideas

1. What might you see in the day sky?

2. What might you see in the night sky?

3. Tell why the sun looks small.

4. Name a group of stars that makes a picture.

Make a mural.

Materials

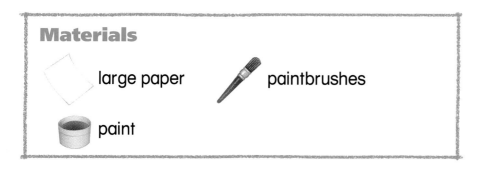

large paper   paintbrushes

paint

1 Choose day or night.

2 Think about what you might see in the day sky or night sky.

3 Make a mural.

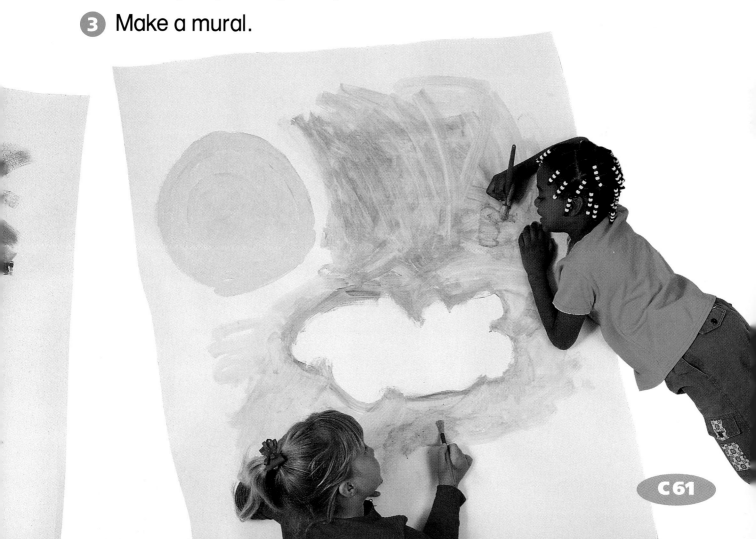

Unit C
Performance Review

There are many places on the earth to visit. Pretend you took an imaginary trip. Where did you go? What was the weather like there? What was it like during the day and at night?

Plan your imaginary trip.

1. Choose a project.

2. Think of what you need to do your project.

3. How will your project tell others about the earth, weather, and the sky?

Make a photo album.

Draw pictures of places you saw on your imaginary trip. Pretend they are pictures that you took with a camera. Put the pictures in a book about your trip.

Write a weather report.

Make a chart that shows what the weather was like in the place that you visited. Show the weather for each day. Tell others what to wear if they go to the same place.

Pretend you are a reporter.

Ask your friends questions about their imaginary trip. Ask where they went and what they saw. Think of more questions to ask.

Writing a Story

A story tells about something that happened. When you write a story, you can tell about where it happened. You can also tell who was there. A story can be real or imaginary.

1. **Prewrite** Choose a place. It can be a mountain, beach, waterfall, or other place on the earth. Draw a picture of it. Think about taking a trip to that place.

2. **Draft** Write a story about the trip. Tell what you did and what you saw.

3. **Revise** Read your story. Do you like it? Make changes if you want to.

4. **Edit** Check your writing to make sure it is correct. Make a neat copy.

5. **Publish** Share your story and picture with others.

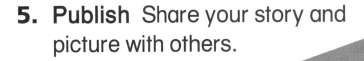

Unit D
Human Body

Science and Technology
In Your World!

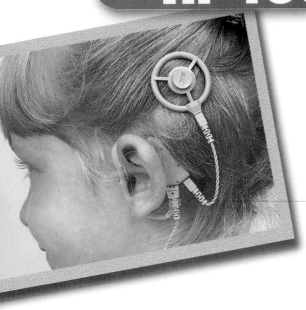

What can a bionic ear do?

It can help children who have impaired hearing. When the children hear how words sound they can learn to talk.

Chapter 1
The Senses

How can light help your teeth?

A laser is a special light. Dentists can use a laser to get rid of cavities that hurt teeth.

Chapter 2
Growing and Changing

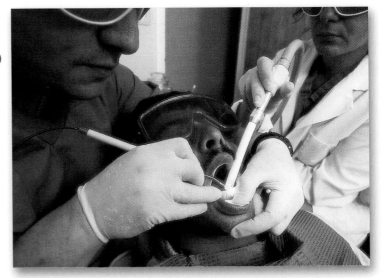

How does a bicycle helmet protect you?

Most helmets have foam inside. The foam is covered with strong plastic. The foam and plastic protect your head in case you fall.

Chapter 3
Taking Care of Your Health

Chapter 1
The Senses

Something Cooking

 Sing to the tune of *If You're Happy and You Know It, Clap Your Hands.*

You can smell there's something cooking,
Use your nose.
You can see they're apple muffins,
Use your eyes.
With your nose, you smell what's cooking.
With your eyes you see they're muffins.
All your senses let you know what's going on.

With your ears you hear the timer,
When they're done.
With your fingers you can touch them.
Are they cool?
With your ears you hear the timer,
With your fingers you can touch them.
All your senses let you know what's going on.

Take a muffin, take a bite.
Mmm, it's good!
With your tongue, you taste the muffin.
Mmm, it's good!
When you bite into a muffin,
It's your tongue that helps you taste it.
All your senses let you know what's going on.

What can you observe?

Look at all the soap bubbles. Is the water warm enough? It's bath time for this dog!

What do you do when you observe? When you **observe**, you notice many things. Observing helps you learn about things.

What do these people see? What do they hear? What else might they observe?

Tell what is in the bag.

Materials

   classroom objects

 paper bag

Process Skills

- observing
- inferring

Steps

1. Take turns with a partner.

2. Close your eyes. Have your partner put an object in the bag.

3. Without looking, reach into the bag and **observe** how the object feels.

4. **Infer.** What is the object?

Share. Draw what you think is in the bag. Then look in the bag.

Lesson Review

1. If you were washing a dog, what might you observe?

2. Tell about something you observe in the classroom.

3. **Tell** what you observed about the object in the bag.

Reading Captions

A caption is a sentence that tells about a picture. An arrow points to the picture that goes with the caption.

Find the caption for the picture of the dog. What does it say?

▲ This dog uses its nose to follow a squirrel.

Read the caption for each picture.

▲ Big ears help this deer hear.

An eagle uses its eyes to
see a fish from very far away. ▶

Turn the page to read
more captions.

Turn the
page.

What are the five senses?

What can you use to observe all the things around you?

You can use your **senses** to observe. You have five senses. Your senses are seeing, hearing, smelling, touching, and tasting.

Your ears help you **hear** . ▼

▲ Your eyes help you **see** .

▲ Your tongue helps you **taste**.

▲ You **touch** things with your skin.

Your nose helps you **smell**. ▼

Lesson Review

1. What are the five senses?

2. What part of your body helps you hear?

3. **Draw** a picture of yourself using one of your senses.

What sounds do you hear?

Process Skills

- observing
- inferring

Materials

 containers with lids

 index cards

   classroom objects

Steps

1. Shake a container. **Observe** the sound.

2. **Infer.** Find the card that tells what you think is in the container.

3. Use a chart like the one in the picture. Record what you think is in the container.

4. Open the container. Record.

5. Do it again.

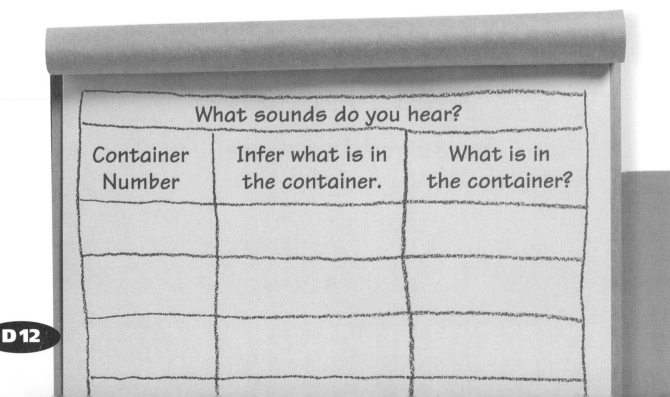

What sounds do you hear?		
Container Number	Infer what is in the container.	What is in the container?

Think About Your Results

1. How could you tell what was in the containers?

2. Which sounds were hard to identify?

 Inquire Further

What could you put in a container that makes a loud sound? What could you put in that makes a soft sound?

Experiment with sight.

Process Skills	Materials
• experimenting • collecting and interpreting data (record)	safety goggles with one side covered ball

Problem

Can you see better with one eye or two eyes?

Give Your Hypothesis

If you cover one eye, will you catch more or fewer balls? Tell what you think.

Control the Variables

Make sure your partner tosses the ball from the same place each time.

Test Your Hypothesis

Follow these steps to do the **experiment**.

1 Work with a partner.

2 Have your partner toss the ball to you 10 times. Count the number of times you catch it.

3 Now put on the safety goggles with one side covered.

4 Have your partner toss the ball to you 10 times. Count the number of times you catch it.

Collect Your Data

Record the number of times you caught the ball using one eye and two eyes.

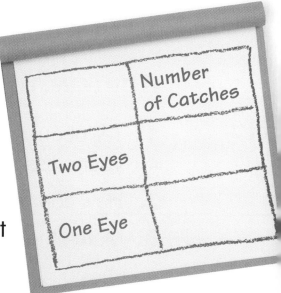

	Number of Catches
Two Eyes	
One Eye	

Tell Your Conclusion

Compare your results and hypothesis. Can you see better with one eye or two eyes?

Inquire Further

Is it easier to catch the ball with the left or the right eye covered?

Chapter 1 Review

Reviewing Science Words

1. Tell about something you **observe** in your classroom.

2. How can your **senses** help you?

3. Match the picture to the word.

see

hear

touch

smell

taste

a

b

c

d

e

Reviewing Science Ideas

1. What senses do you use when you eat a meal?

2. Pretend you are about to cross the street. Tell what senses might help you.

Put on a play.

Materials

sense cards

1 Work with a group.

2 Make up a play. Your play must show all the senses.

3 Perform your play for the class.

4 Have the class hold up sense cards to tell which senses you act out in your play.

Chapter 2
Growing and Changing

Could It Be Me?

♪ Sing to the tune of *Hush Little Baby*.

I'm looking at a photo and could it be,
That this little baby grew up to be me!
There's not much hair on this baby's head
But mine's long and curly and very red.

And this little baby's crawling around
But I can ride a bike and walk to town.
In another photo I can see
I used to be as tall as my father's knee.

But now when I stand up next to Dad
My head's at his elbow, that makes me glad.
And if I keep growing in every way
Will I be bigger than Dad some day?

Original lyrics by Gerri Brioso and Richard Freitas.
Produced by Children's Television Workshop.
Copyright ©1999 Sesame Street, Inc.

How have you grown?

Think about how you looked when you were a baby. How big were you? What did you do?

When you were a baby, you could not talk or walk. You crawled from place to place. You may have cried a lot and slept a lot.

You have grown and changed in many ways. You are taller. You can walk, run, and jump. In what other ways have you changed?

6 years

5 years

4 years

3 years

See how you have grown.

Materials

 baby picture

 recent picture

Process Skills

- observing
- predicting

Process Skills

Steps

1. **Observe** your baby picture.

2. **Observe** how you look now.

3. Think about how you have grown.

4. **Predict** how you might change as you grow older.

Share. Write about how you have grown.

Lesson Review

1. What are some things that babies do?

2. Tell two ways you might change as you grow older.

3. **Draw** something you can do now that you could not do when you were younger.

Estimating and Measuring

You can measure to find out how long something is. This crayon is about 9 centimeters long.

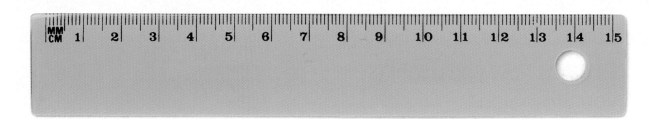

About how long are the eraser and pencil? Measure to find out.

You can estimate before you measure. When you estimate, you tell how long you think something is. About how long do you think the marker is? Estimate. Then measure to find out.

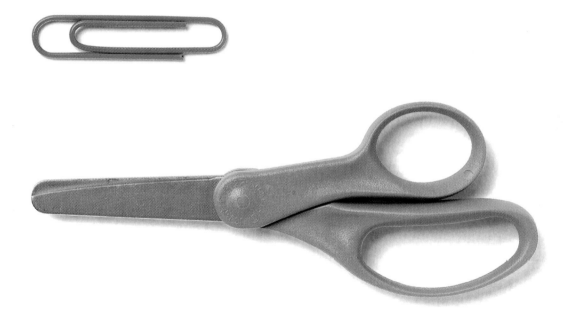

Estimate then measure the paper clip and the scissors.

Turn the page for an activity about estimating and measuring.

Turn the page.

How can you measure your body?

Process Skills

- estimating and measuring

Materials

tape measure

Steps

1. **Estimate** the length of your foot. Record on a chart like this one.

2. **Measure** the length of your foot. Record.

3. Estimate and then measure the length of your hand, arm, and other body parts. Record.

Foot

Estimate. _____ centimeters

Measure. _____ centimeters

Hand

Estimate. _____ centimeters

Measure. _____ centimeters

Think About Your Results

1. Which is longer, your hand or your foot?

2. What can you measure on your body that is less than 5 centimeters long?

 **Inquire Further**

Which is longer, your arm span or your height?

How do teeth grow and change?

You see them when you smile. You use them when you chew. Sometimes you lose them. What are they?

A baby is born with no teeth showing. Soon, first teeth begin to grow.

This girl has many first teeth. Permanent teeth grow and push out first teeth. Have you lost your front teeth like the girl in the picture?

You see permanent teeth in this boy's smile. If you take care of permanent teeth, they can last your whole life.

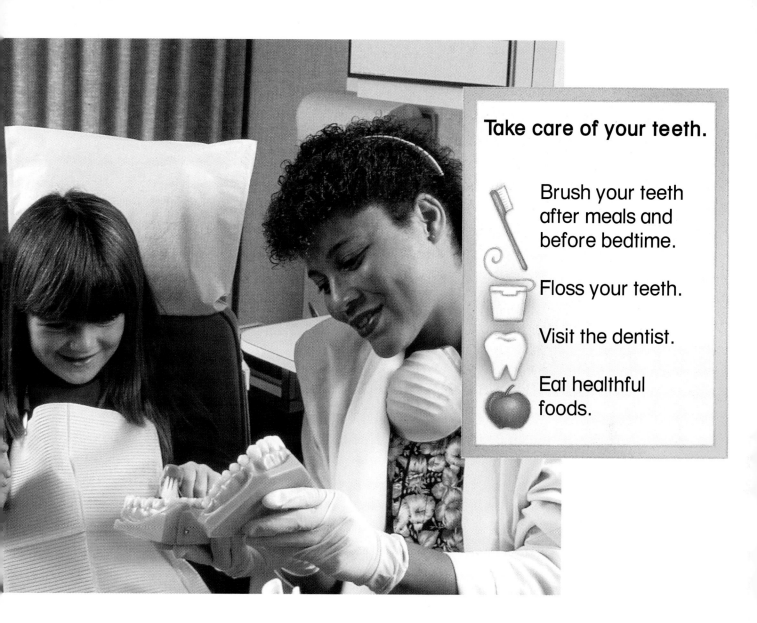

Take care of your teeth.

Brush your teeth after meals and before bedtime.

Floss your teeth.

Visit the dentist.

Eat healthful foods.

Lesson Review

1. How many first teeth have you lost?

2. What pushes out first teeth?

3. **Write** a list of ways to take care of your teeth.

What do bones and muscles do?

Stand up. Turn around. Touch your nose. Sit down. What makes your body move?

Your body has many muscles. **Muscles** help your body move. You use muscles in your arms and hands when you catch a ball. Muscles also help you smile. Put your hands on your cheeks. Smile. You can feel the muscles in your face move!

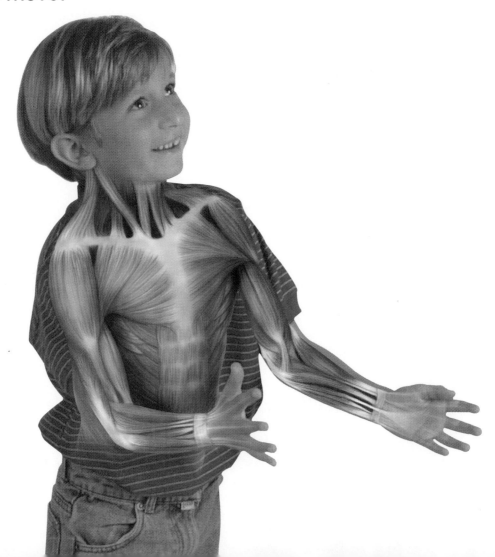

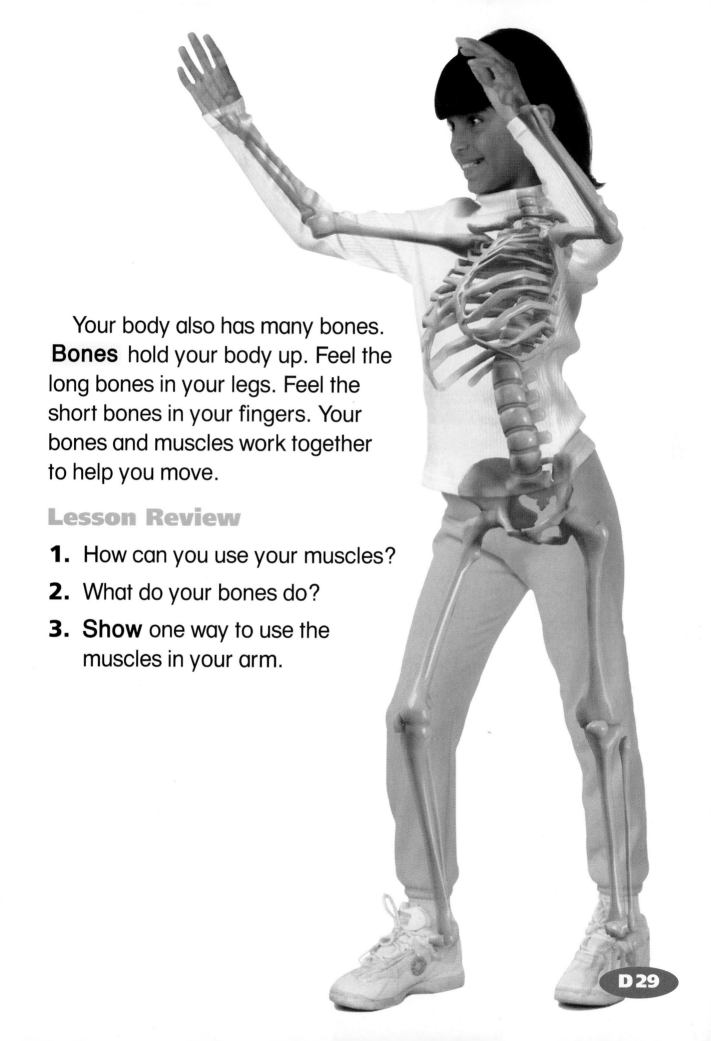

Your body also has many bones. **Bones** hold your body up. Feel the long bones in your legs. Feel the short bones in your fingers. Your bones and muscles work together to help you move.

Lesson Review

1. How can you use your muscles?

2. What do your bones do?

3. **Show** one way to use the muscles in your arm.

Chapter 2 Review

Reviewing Science Words

1. What do your **muscles** do?

2. What do your **bones** do?

Reviewing Science Ideas

1. Tell how you have changed since you were a baby.

2. What four things can you do to take care of your teeth?

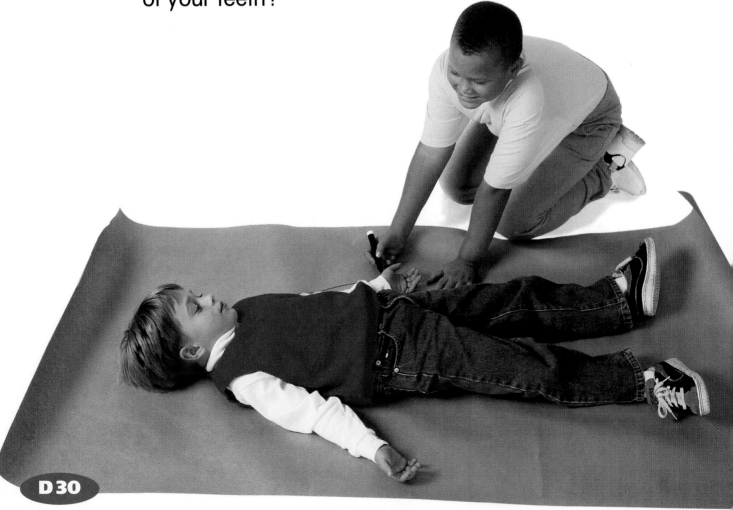

Trace and draw your body.

Materials

large paper   crayons

1. Lie on a large piece of paper.
2. Have your partner trace around your body.
3. Draw teeth in your mouth.
4. Draw your bones.
5. Draw muscles in your arms.

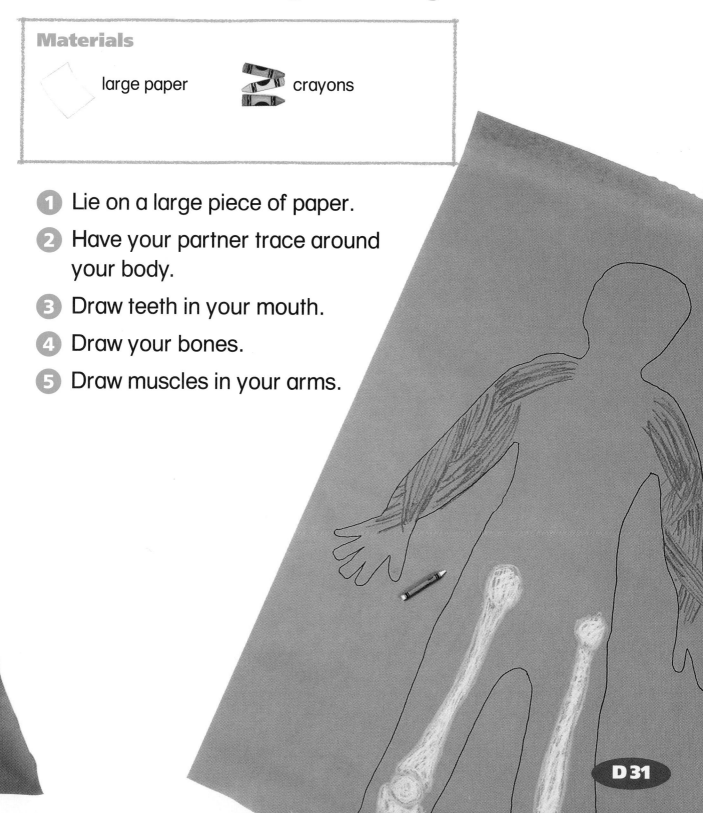

Taking Care of Your Health

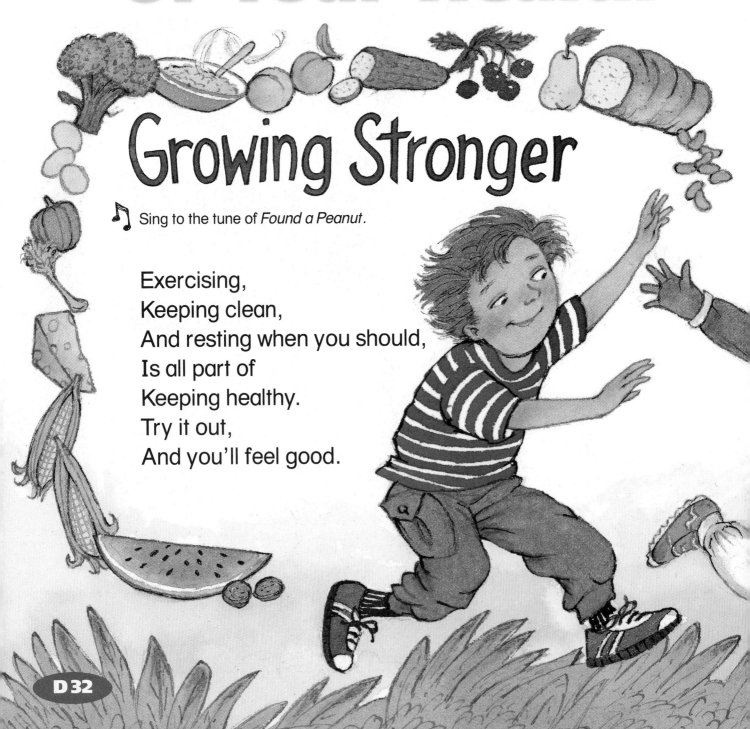

Growing Stronger

♪ Sing to the tune of *Found a Peanut*.

Exercising,
Keeping clean,
And resting when you should,
Is all part of
Keeping healthy.
Try it out,
And you'll feel good.

Eat some good food.
Choose it wisely,
From the healthy foods we know,
Rice and milk, meat,
Fruit and vegetables,
Are some foods
That help you grow.

It's important,
To keep healthy,
If you want to run and play.
Keeping healthy,
Keeps your body,
Growing stronger everyday.

What foods help you grow?

You need food to grow. Which foods will help you stay healthy?

The **Food Guide Pyramid** shows groups of food. There are six groups in the Food Guide Pyramid. What kinds of foods are in each group?

You need to eat more food from the bottom of the Food Guide Pyramid. You need to eat less food from the top.

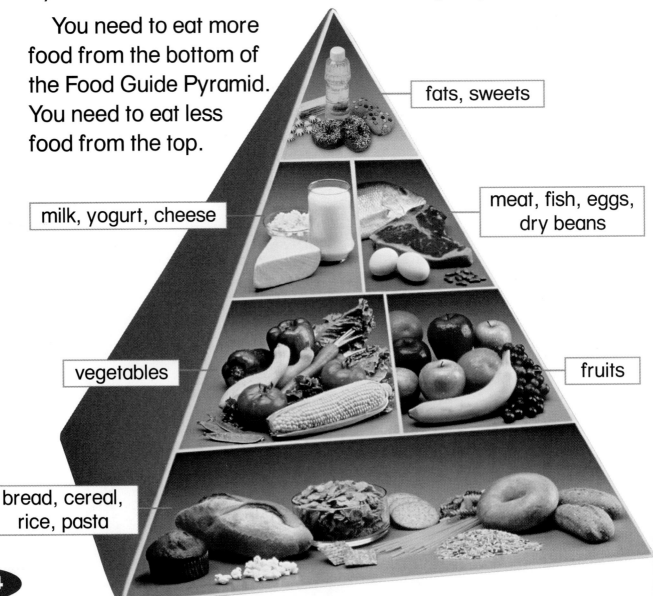

fats, sweets

meat, fish, eggs, dry beans

milk, yogurt, cheese

vegetables

fruits

bread, cereal, rice, pasta

Classify foods.

Materials

 paper  pencil  crayons

- classifying

Process Skills

Steps

1. Make a Food Guide Pyramid.

2. Label each food group.

3. Think of foods to **classify.**
   Draw one food for each group.

Share. Name a favorite food from each group in the Food Guide Pyramid.

Lesson Review

1. What part of the Food Guide Pyramid shows food you should eat most?

2. What part of the Food Guide Pyramid shows food you should eat least?

3. **Tell** how you can eat healthier foods.

How can you stay healthy?

Do you like to play tag or balance on one foot? Do you like to fly through the air on a swing or go down a slide?

Playing and moving are ways to **exercise**. Exercise helps you stay healthy. When you jump rope or do a somersault you are exercising. What other ways can you play that give you exercise?

Staying clean also keeps you healthy. Germs can get on your hands. Wash your hands before you eat. Wash them after you touch a pet or use a restroom.

You also need sleep to keep healthy. Sleep helps you work and play. You need eight to ten hours of sleep every night.

Lesson Review

1. What are some things you can do to stay healthy?

2. When should you wash your hands?

3. **Draw** a picture that shows your favorite way to get exercise.

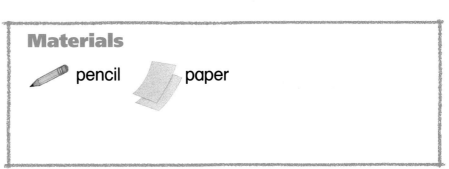

Is it easier to balance with eyes open or closed?

Process Skills

- predicting
- observing
- making definitions

Materials

pencil   paper

Steps

1. **Predict.** When you stand on one foot, is it easier to balance with your eyes open or closed? Record.

2. Stand on one foot. **Observe.** How easy is it?

3. Now close your eyes. Stand on one foot. **Observe.** How easy is it? Record.

4. **Predict** again. When you stand on your toes, is it easier to balance with your eyes open or closed? Record.

5. Stand on your toes. **Observe.** How easy is it?

6. Now close your eyes. Stand on your toes. **Observe.** How easy is it? Record.

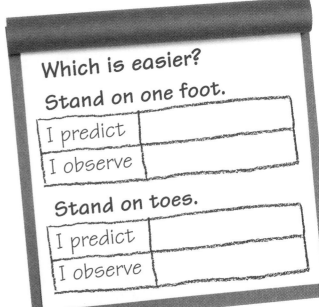

Which is easier?

Stand on one foot.

I predict	
I observe	

Stand on toes.

I predict	
I observe	

Think About Your Results

1. **Make a definition.** Tell what the word **balance** means.

2. Do you balance better with your eyes open or closed?

 Inquire Further

How can you improve your balance?

Using Pictures

You can learn a lot from looking at pictures.
This picture shows a playground that is safe.

Tell how this playground is different from the playground on the other page. What would you do to make this playground more safe?

Turn the page to learn more about staying safe.

Turn the page.

How can you stay safe?

Imagine you are at a busy corner. How can you cross the street safely?

When you cross the street, make sure no cars are coming. Look left, right, and left again. Cross when it is safe. A traffic light or crossing guard can help you.

The children in this picture are waiting to cross the street. White lines on the street show the safest place to walk. This place is called the **crosswalk**.

Find other ways people in this picture are staying safe. What do you observe about the girl with the bicycle or the person in the car? Tell about other ways to stay safe outdoors, at home, and at school.

Lesson Review

1. What should you do before you cross the street?

2. Where is a safe place to cross the street?

3. **Draw** a picture that shows how to stay safe outdoors, at home, or at school.

Chapter 3 Review

Reviewing Science Words

1. What does the **Food Guide Pyramid** show?

2. Name three ways to **exercise**.

3. What is a **crosswalk**?

Reviewing Science Ideas

1. From which group in the Food Guide Pyramid do you need to eat the most food?

2. When should you wash your hands?

3. Tell how to cross the street safely.

Make a mobile.

1. Draw a big picture of yourself.

2. Use cards. Draw healthy foods. Draw ways to exercise, rest, and stay clean. Draw ways to stay safe.

3. Tape yarn to each card. Tape the cards to the big picture.

Unit D Performance Review

You have learned why your senses are important and how to take care of your health. You have learned about growing and changing, too. Have a health fair to show others what you have learned.

Plan your health fair.

1. Pick a project you would like to do.

2. Decide how you will do your project.

3. How will your project tell others about the senses, growing, and health?

Write a poem.

Write a poem about the five senses. Use all five senses in your poem. You can use the words see, hear, touch, taste, and smell.

Play charades.

Think of words that tell about the senses, growing, and health. Write each word on a card. Put the cards into a bag. Choose a card. Act out the word. See if others can guess the word. Take turns.

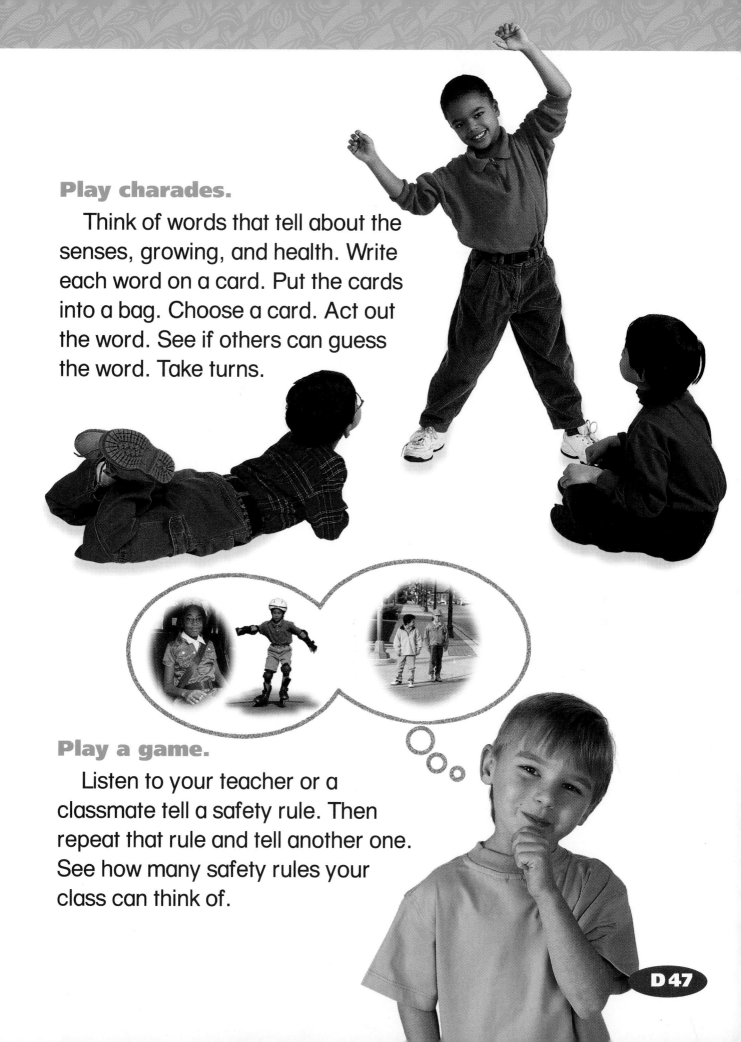

Play a game.

Listen to your teacher or a classmate tell a safety rule. Then repeat that rule and tell another one. See how many safety rules your class can think of.

Writing About How to Stay Healthy

When you get people to do something, you persuade them. You can also persuade people that something is important. You can make a poster to persuade people. You can draw pictures and write sentences on your poster.

1. **Prewrite** Think of something you can do to stay healthy. Draw a picture on your poster.

2. **Draft** How can you persuade others to follow your idea? Write sentences that tell why your idea a good one.

3. **Revise** Read what you wrote. Will it persuade others to follow your idea?

4. **Edit** Check your writing to make sure it is correct. Copy it onto your poster.

5. **Publish** Share your poster with others. Ask what they think about your idea. Did you persuade them to follow your idea?

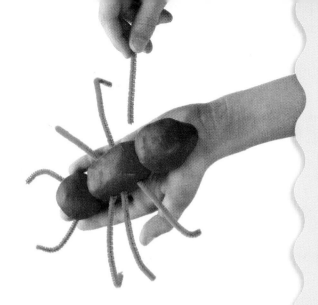

Your Science Handbook

⚠️ Safety in Science

Scientists do their experiments safely. You need to be careful when doing experiments too. The next page includes some safety tips to remember.

- Read each experiment carefully.
- Wear safety goggles when needed.
- Clean up spills right away.
- Never taste or smell materials unless your teacher tells you to.
- Tape sharp edges of materials.
- Put things away when you finish an experiment.
- Wash your hands after each experiment.

Using the Metric System

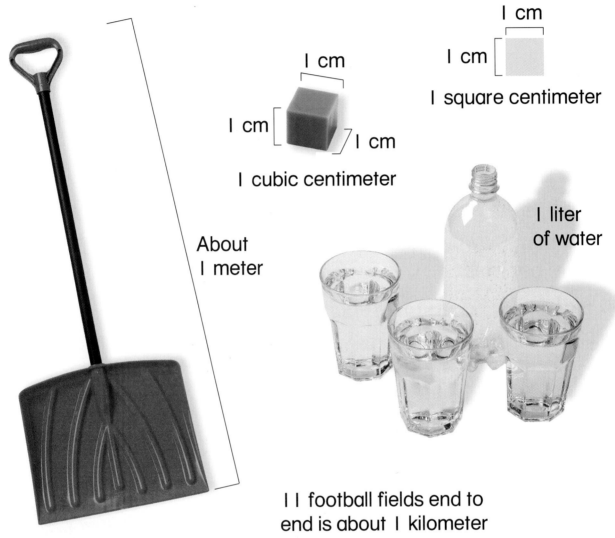

1 cm

1 cm

1 cm

1 cubic centimeter

1 cm

1 cm

1 square centimeter

About
1 meter

1 liter
of water

11 football fields end to
end is about 1 kilometer

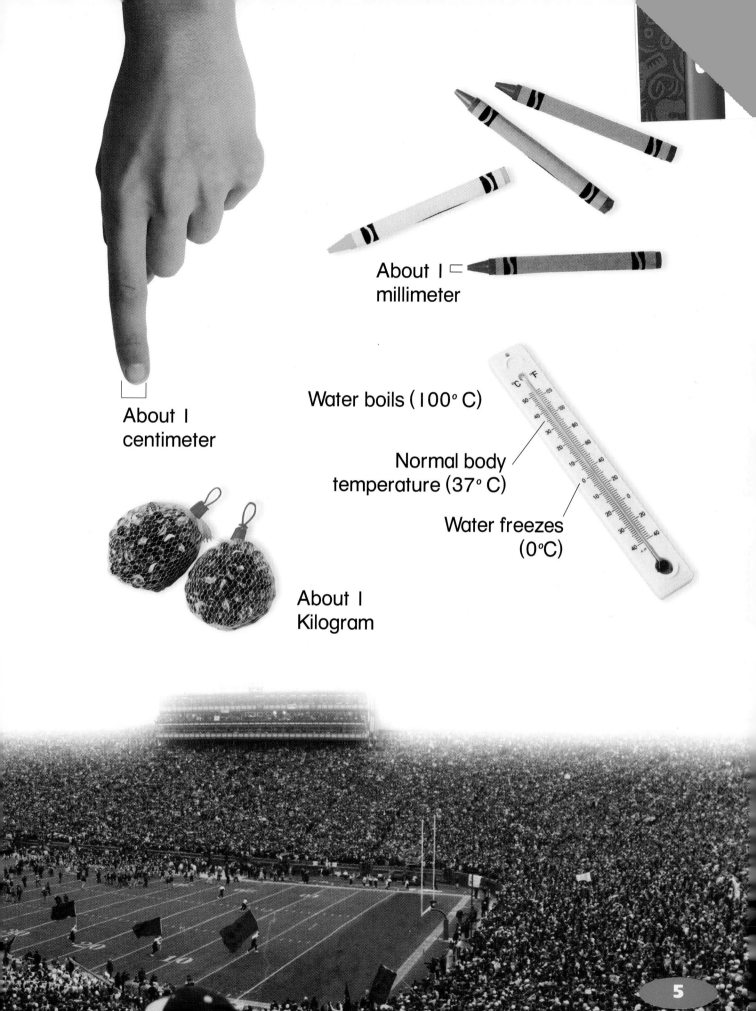

About 1
millimeter

About 1
centimeter

Water boils (100° C)

Normal body
temperature (37° C)

Water freezes
(0°C)

About 1
Kilogram

5

Observing

How do you observe?

You observe with your five senses. You observe when your eyes see and when your ears hear. You observe when your fingers and body touch things. You observe when your nose smells and your tongue tastes. Only foods should go in your mouth!

Practice Observing

Materials

 hand lens  4 walnuts

Follow these steps

1 Make a chart like this one.

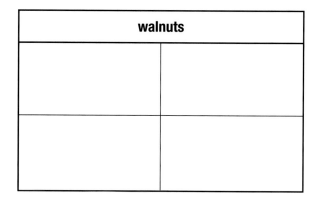

walnuts	

2 Put one walnut in each box of the chart.

3 Observe each walnut with the hand lens.

4 Write what you observe in the box.

5 Draw a picture of each walnut.

6 Take the walnuts out of each box.

Thinking About Your Thinking

Is each walnut a little different from the others? How are they different? Have a friend try to put each walnut in the right box. Have your friend tell how they are different.

Communicating

How do you communicate?

You communicate when you talk. You also communicate when you draw a picture, write a story, act something out, make a graph, or even sing a song.

Practice Communicating

Materials

 paper    crayons

Follow these steps

1. Look at pictures of a stream, river, lake, and ocean.

2. Draw your own picture of a stream, river, lake and ocean.

3. Share your pictures with your class.

4. Describe each picture.

Thinking About Your Thinking

What other ways could you communicate to your classmates about what a stream, river, lake, or ocean is.

Classifying

What does it mean to classify things?

You classify things when you group them by what they have in common. Shape, color, and texture are some ways to classify things. There are often different ways to classify the same things.

Practice Classifying

Materials

 colored blocks of different sizes

Follow these steps

1 Work with a partner.

2 Classify the blocks by color.

3 Classify the blocks again. This time classify by shape.

4 Think of another way to classify the blocks.

Thinking About Your Thinking

Choose some objects. Think of new ways to classify them.

Estimating and Measuring

What is estimating and measuring?

You can estimate before you measure. When you estimate you tell how long, tall, wide, or heavy you think something is. After you make an estimate, you can check it by measuring the object.

Practice Estimating and Measuring

Materials

 Snap Cubes ruler

Follow these steps

 Make a chart like the one below.

How many Snap Cubes long?		
Object	Estimate	Measure

2 Choose an object. About how many Snap Cubes long does it look? Make an estimate. Measure the object. Record.

3 Make a chart like this one.

How many centimeters long?		
Object	Estimate	Measure

4 About how many centimeters long does your object look?

5 Repeat the activity with other objects.

Thinking About Your Thinking

How is measuring length with centimeters like measuring length with cubes? How is it different?

Inferring

What does it mean to infer?

You infer when you make a conclusion or a guess from what you observe or from what you already know. You can infer from what you observe with your five senses.

Practice Inferring

Materials

 16 pinto beans   3 containers with lids

Follow these steps

1 Put 1 bean in a container. Put 5 beans in another container. Put 10 beans in another container.

2 Have your partner shake each container.

3 Ask your partner to infer which container has 1 bean, 5 beans, and 10 beans.

4 Have your partner put the containers in order from the least beans to the most beans.

5 Mix up the containers. Trade places and do the activity again.

Thinking About Your Thinking

Which senses did you use to infer which container had the fewest and most beans?

Predicting

How do you predict?

When you predict, you tell what you think will happen. If you observe something carefully first, it will help you to make better predictions.

Practice Predicting

Materials

 10 paper clips   10 lima beans

Follow these steps

1 Make a chart like the one below.

Patterns				

2 Use the paper clips and lima beans.

3 Make a pattern that fills 4 boxes in a row.

4 Have your partner predict what goes in the next box.

5 Have your partner start a pattern. Predict how to complete the pattern.

Thinking About Your Thinking

What process skill can
help you finish the pattern?

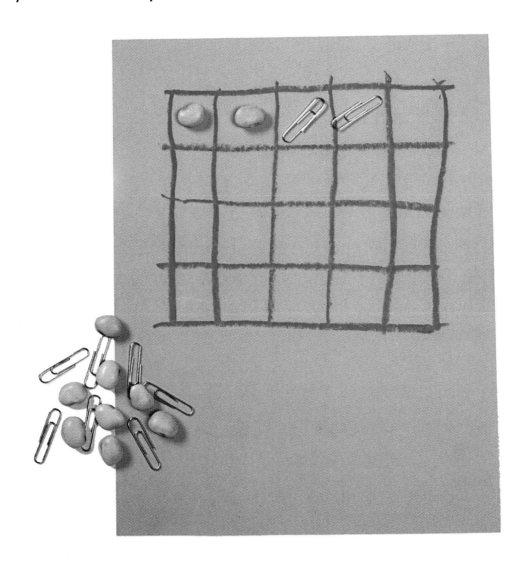

Making Definitions

How can you make a definition?

A definition tells what something means. You can use something you know or something you do to make a definition for a word.

Practice Making Definitions

Materials

 books   ruler

 small block

Follow these steps

1. Build a ramp with books and a ruler.

2. Tell what you notice about the ramp. Is it smooth? Is it level? How have you seen ramps used? How can you use a ramp?

3 Put the block at the top of the ramp. Let the block slide down the ramp.

4 Make a definition for the word **ramp**.

5 Find the definition of **ramp** in the dictionary. Write it down.

Thinking About Your Thinking

Compare your definition with the dictionary definition. How were they alike? How were they different? Do you think the block would move if it was on a flat ruler rather than the ramp? Why or why not?

Making and Using Models

What can you do with a model?

You can use a model to show what you know about something. A model can also help others learn about the thing that the model represents.

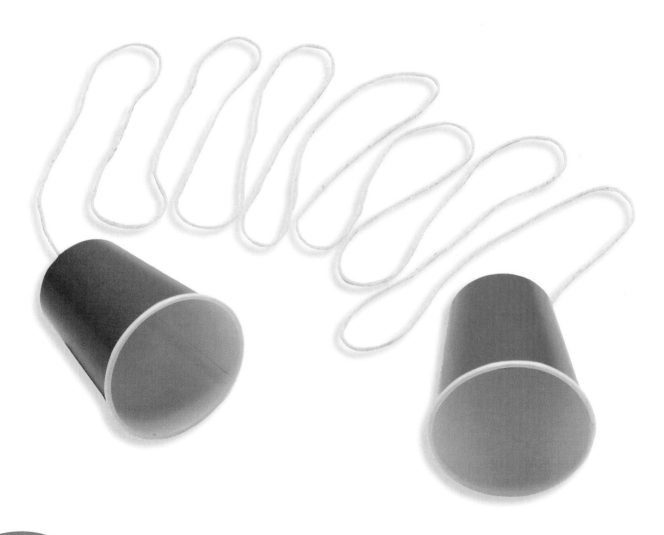

Practice Making and Using Models

Materials

 2 paper cups   string

 safety goggles

 2 paper clips   pencil

Follow these steps

1 Put on your safety goggles.

2 Use the tip of your pencil to poke a small hole in the bottom of each cup.

3 Put the ends of the string through each cup.

4 Tie a paper clip to the end of each string.

5 Have your partner hold one cup as you hold the other cup. Step back until the string is tight.

6 Have your partner talk into the cup. Can you hear what your partner is saying? Take turns talking and listening.

Thinking About Your Thinking

How is your model like a telephone?
How is it different?

Giving Hypotheses

Why do you ask questions and give hypotheses?

You can ask questions to try to understand something. When you give a hypothesis, you make a statement. Then you can test it to see if it is correct.

Practice Giving Hypotheses

Materials

○ cotton ball   wooden block

Follow these steps

1. If you blow on a cotton ball and a wooden block with the same force, which will move farther? Tell what you think. This is your hypothesis.

2. Test the hypothesis. Place the cotton ball and the block on your desk.

3. Do the experiment. Blow on the cotton ball. Blow on the block.

Thinking About Your Thinking

Which object went further, the cotton ball or wooden block? Did your results match your hypothesis? What other questions do you have?

Collecting Data

How do you collect and interpret data?

You collect data when you record what you observe. You can use pictures, words, graphs, or charts to display data.

You interpret data when you use what you have learned to explain something or answer a question.

Practice Collecting Data

Materials

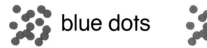 blue dots    red dots

 yellow dots   green dots

Follow these steps

blue	red	yellow	green

1 Make a bar graph like this one.

2 Choose a different number of dots for each color.

3 Put blue dots in the column marked **blue**. Put red dots in the column marked **red**.

4 Do the same with your yellow and green dots.

5 Count the dots in each column. Write the number in the circle below each column.

Thinking About Your Thinking

How many of each color dot did you put in your bar graph? Which column had the most dots? Which column had the fewest?

Controlling Variables

What does it mean to control variables?

You control variables when you do an activity and change just one thing. The thing you change is called the variable.

A variable can be almost anything. It can be distance, or light, or temperature. Only one variable changes at a time.

Practice Identifying and Controlling Variables

Materials

 safety goggles   shoe box

 3 rubber bands of different thicknesses

Follow these steps

1 Put on your safety goggles.

2 Stretch I rubber band over the shoebox. Pluck the rubber band. Was the sound high or low?

3 Stretch another rubber band over the shoe box. Pluck the rubber band. How did the sound compare to the first rubber band?

4 Repeat step 2 with the third rubber band. How did this sound compare with the others?

Thinking About Your Thinking

What is the variable in this activity? What things did not change?

Experimenting

How do you experiment?

When you do an experiment, you follow a plan to answer a question. When you are finished, you make conclusions about what you have learned.

Practice Experimenting

Materials

 2 cups of water   salt   sand

       plastic spoon

Follow these steps

Problem

What happens to the salt and sand when they are put in water?

Give Your Hypothesis

If you put salt in water and sand in water, which will dissolve? Tell what you think.

Control the Variables

Use the same amount of water and the same temperature of water in both cups.

Test Your Hypothesis

Follow these steps to do the experiment.

1. Label one cup **salt** and the other **sand**.

2. Add water to both cups.

3. Add 2 spoonfuls of salt to the water. Predict. What will happen to the salt? Stir the saltwater for 30 seconds.

4. Add 2 spoonfuls of sand to the other cup. Predict. What will happen the sand? Stir the sand and water for 30 seconds.

Collect Your Data

Draw two pictures. Draw the sand and salt before the experiment. Draw the sand and salt after you stirred them in the water.

Tell Your Conclusion

Compare your results and hypothesis. What happened to the salt and the sand when you added them to the water?

Thinking About Your Thinking

Was your hypothesis correct?
Why or why not?

Endangered Plants and Animals

Some plants and animals are endangered. That means that very few of them are living. People all over the world are working to protect many endangered plants and animals.

Endangered Plants

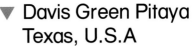 Eureka Valley Evening Primrose California, U.S.A.

▼ Davis Green Pitaya Texas, U.S.A

▲ Western Lily Oregon, U.S.A.

Endangered Animals

▲ Snow Leopard
Tibet

Orangutan
Borneo and Sumatra ▲

Green Sea Turtle
Hawaii, U.S.A. ▼

Terrariums

A terrarium is a container with soil in it. It has plants in it. It can also have animals, such as lizards, toads, salamanders, and snakes. A lid on top keeps enough water inside. A terrarium is a habitat that has everything the plants and animals need.

Aquariums

Aquariums have water in them. Fish can live in an aquarium. People take care of the fish by feeding them and keeping the water clean. Snails and plants can live in an aquarium too. An aquarium is a habitat that has everything they need.

The thermometer shows how warm the water is.

The heater keeps the water warm.

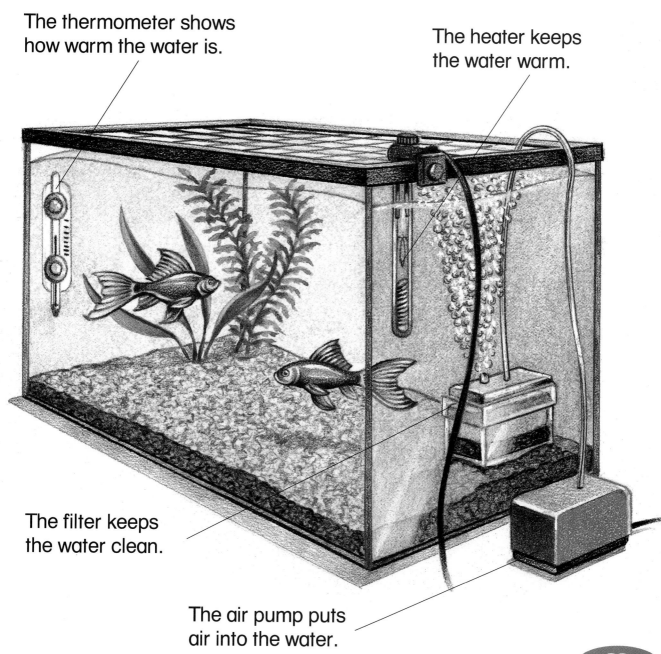

The filter keeps the water clean.

The air pump puts air into the water.

Using Graphs

Are there more black, orange, or striped fish in the tank? A graph can help you compare the groups. These pages show three kinds of graphs.

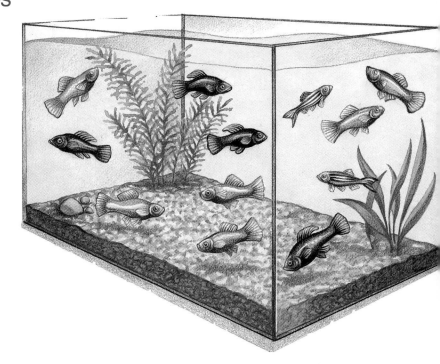

Picture Graph

This graph uses pictures. How many fish are in each group?

Fish

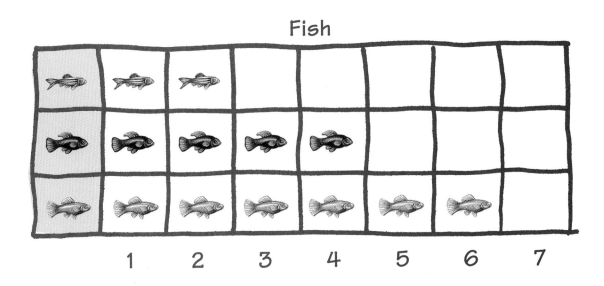

1   2   3   4   5   6   7

Bar Graph

In this bar graph, one box is filled for each fish. How many more orange fish are there than striped fish?

Fish

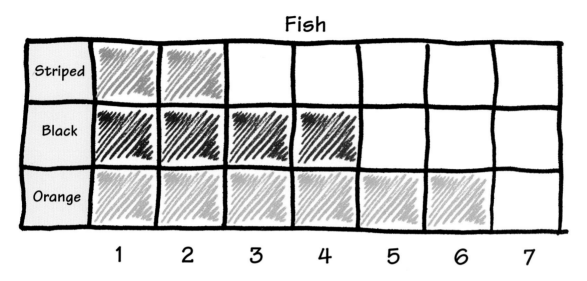

| | 1 | 2 | 3 | 4 | 5 | 6 | 7 |

Circle Graph

This circle graph shows that there are 2 striped fish and 4 black fish. How many orange fish are there?

Fish

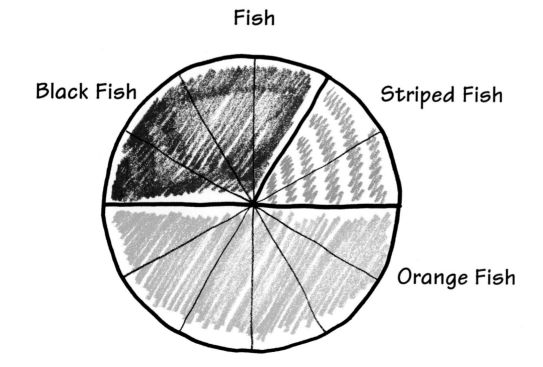

Fossils

The pictures on this page show three different fossils. A fossil is a part of or a print of a plant or animal that lived long ago.

Stegosaurus

Tyrannosaurus rex

fern

Dinosaurs

Scientists have learned about many kinds of dinosaurs by studying fossils. They know that some dinosaurs ate plants and others ate meat. Read to find out what these dinosaurs ate.

Triceratops ate plants.

Stegosaurus ate plants.

Compsognathus ate meat.

Tyrannosaurus ate meat.

Electricity

All objects have tiny bits of electricity called electric charges. Rubbing objects together can cause these electric charges to move from one object to another.

This girl is rubbing a balloon on her wool sweater. The balloon picks up electric charges from the sweater. These electric charges cause the balloon to stick to the wall.

Electricity can be stored in a battery. The electric charges move through the battery. They move in a path called a circuit. When the circuit is complete, the bulb lights up.

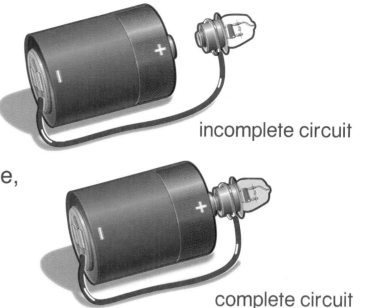

incomplete circuit

complete circuit

You use electricity in your home. When you plug in a lamp, electric charges move from the outlet through the lamp cord. Then the circuit is complete and the lamp lights up.

Mixtures and Solutions

When you mix two or more materials together, you make a mixture. This salad is a mixture. You can easily separate each piece.

Some liquids can mix together to make a solution.

This is another kind of mixture. It is a solution. The powdered drink mix dissolves in cold water to make lemonade. Other kinds of powders only dissolve easily in hot water.

Some materials do not mix with water. The oil floats on top of the water. The sand sinks to the bottom.

Water Cycle

Water moving from the clouds to the earth and back to clouds again is called the water cycle.

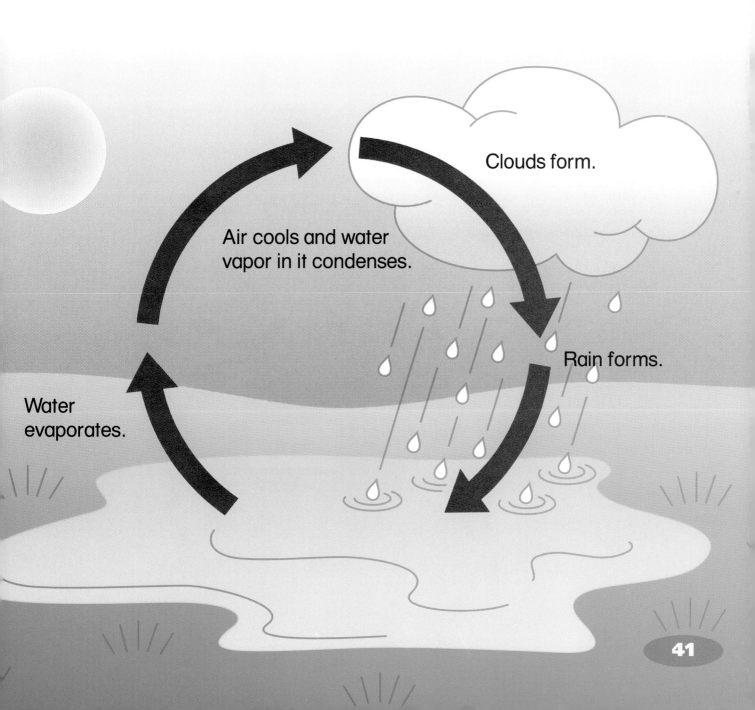

Clouds form.

Air cools and water vapor in it condenses.

Rain forms.

Water evaporates.

Solar System

The sun is the center of our solar system. The planets in our solar system move around the sun.

Name each planet. Count them. How many planets are in our solar system? Which planet is the largest? Which one is closest to the sun?

Jupiter

Mars

Mercury

Venus

Earth

Sun

Saturn

Uranus

Neptune

Pluto

Space Exploration

Scientists use special equipment to learn about space. The Mars Pathfinder was sent to Mars. Astronauts do not travel on the Mars Pathfinder. Cameras, computers, and other equipment record information. The information is sent back to Earth.

Look at the picture of the Space Shuttle. Astronauts who travel on the Space Shuttle do experiments in space. They learn what it is like to live without gravity.

The Mars Pathfinder carried the Sojourner Rover to Mars. The Sojourner Rover collected important information. ▶

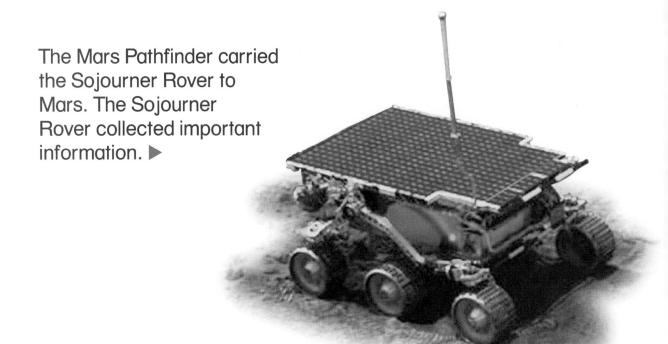

The Digestive System

When you eat, you chew and swallow food. The food goes down a tube called the esophagus. Then it goes into your stomach. Next it is digested in the small intestine. Most digestion happens in the small intestine. Food that is not digested goes into the large intestine. Then it passes out of the body.

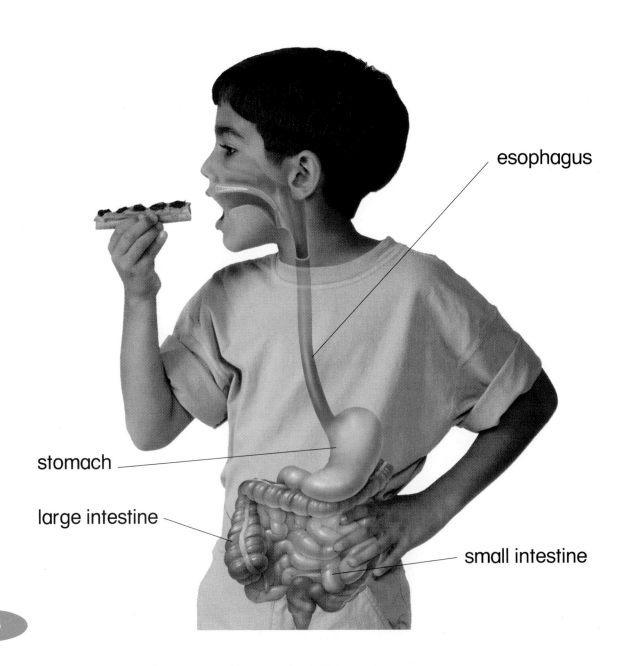

esophagus

stomach

large intestine

small intestine

The Heart and Lungs

When you breathe, your lungs take in air. Air contains oxygen, a gas that your whole body needs.

Your heart pumps blood to every part of your body. Blood is pumped away from your heart in tubes called arteries. It travels back to the heart in tubes called veins.

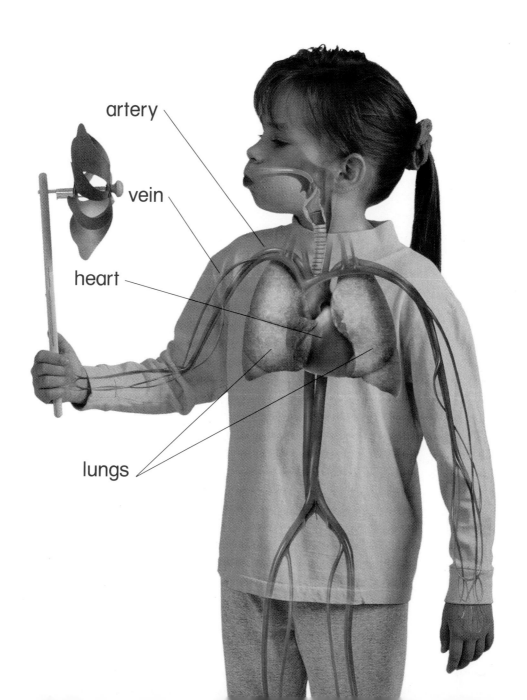

artery

vein

heart

lungs

The Brain and Nervous System

Your brain tells your body what to do. It helps you move, think, feel, and remember. Your brain sends messages through the nerves. Nerves are pathways that lead to and from your brain.

When you see a ball, your brain sends a message. Nerves carry the message to your arm and hand. Your arm and hand move to catch the ball.

brain

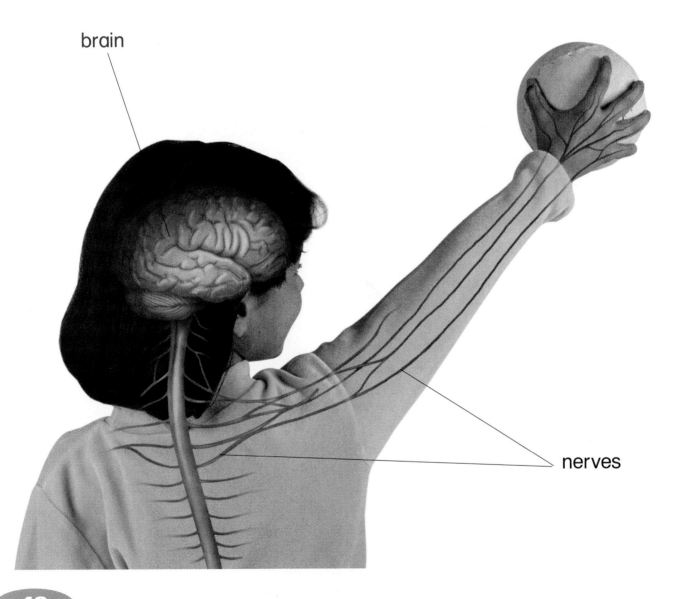

nerves

The Eye

You see things because light travels through your eyes.

1 Light enters the eye through a small opening called the pupil.

4 Messages from the back of the eye follow a path to the brain.

2 Light moves through the lens.

3 Light hits the back of the eye.

Using Measuring Tools

You can use tools to measure how long something is. Most scientists measure length in centimeters or meters.

Measure length with a metric ruler.

1. Find a pencil. Line up the eraser of the pencil with the end of the ruler.

2. Look at the tip of the pencil. Find the centimeter mark that is closest to the tip of the pencil.

3. About how long is the pencil? Record.

Measure length with a meter stick.
What is the length of your classroom?
Measure with a meter stick.

Measure length with a tape measure.
Find something round in your classroom.
Use a tape measure to measure around it.

Using a Thermometer

A thermometer measures the temperature. When the temperature gets warmer, the red line moves up. When it gets cooler, the red line moves down.

Some thermometers have a Celsius and Fahrenheit scale. Most scientists use the Celsius scale.

Measure temperature with a thermometer.

1. Put a thermometer in a cup of cold water.

2. Observe the red line in the thermometer.

3. Put the thermometer in a cup of warm water.

4. Observe the red line again.

5. How did the red line in the thermometer change?

Using a Pan Balance

A pan balance is used to measure mass. Mass is how much matter an object has. Make sure the two sides of a pan balance are level before you use it.

Measure mass with a pan balance.

1. Choose two objects. Which one do you think has more mass?

2. Put an object on each side of the pan balance.

3. Which side of the pan balance is lower? The object on the low side has more mass than the object on the high side.

Using a Hand Lens

You can use a hand lens to make objects look larger than they really are. This helps you see parts of the object that you might not notice without the hand lens.

Observe a penny.

1. Look at a penny through a hand lens.

2. Move the hand lens closer to and farther from the penny. Notice that the penny seems to change size. Notice that the penny can look clear or blurry.

3. Hold the hand lens so that the penny looks clear. Tell what you observe that you did not see without the hand lens.

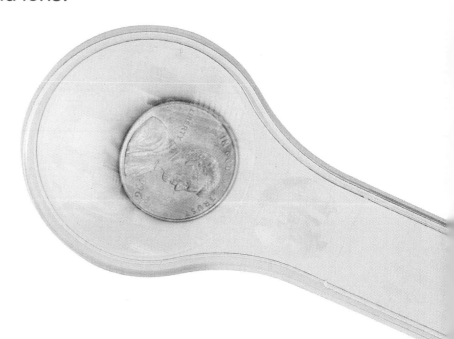

Using a Calculator

A calculator can help you do things, such as add and subtract. This chart shows how much paper a school recycled each month. Use a calculator to figure out how much paper they recycled in all.

1. To add a number, press the number. Then press the ➕ sign.

2. Do this for each number in the chart.

3. When you have added all the numbers, press the ＝ sign.

4. The answer should be 98.

Month	Paper Recycled in kilograms
September	7
October	12
November	13
December	9
January	11
February	14
March	9
April	15
May	8

Using a Computer

You can learn about science at a special Internet website. Go to www.sfscience.com .

1. Use the mouse to click on your grade.

2. Find a topic you would like to learn about. Click on that topic.

3. You can click on an arrow to go to another page. You can also click on words with lines under them.

4. Tell about 3 things that you learned at the website.

Inventions in Science

450 B.C.
People fly the first kites.

250 B.C.
The heavy plow
is invented.

200 B.C.
Archimedes shows how
to use levers and pulleys.

1000 B.C.
People learn to make
tools from iron.

50 B.C.
The wheelbarrow
is invented.

105 A.D.
The first
paper is
made in
China.

375 A.D.	650 A.D.	925 A.D.	1200 A.D.	1475 A.D.

500 A.D.
The first stirrups are used to ride horses.

868 A.D.
The oldest handprinted book is made.

1565 A.D.
The pencil is invented.

550 A.D.
Paper money is made in China.

1150 A.D.
People start to use bars of soap for the first time.

1285 A.D.
Eyeglasses are invented in Italy.

1453 A.D.
The first book is printed with a printing press.

1608 A.D.
The telescope is invented.

1609 A.D.
The first newspaper is printed in Germany.

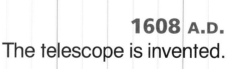

1698 A.D.
Thomas Savery invents the steam engine.

1752
Benjamin Franklin proves that lightning is electricity and invents the lightning rod to protect buildings from lightning.

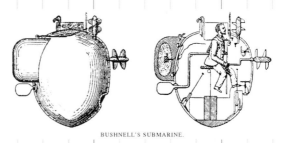

BUSHNELL'S SUBMARINE.

1776
The first submarine is built.

1793
Eli Whitney invents the cotton gin to clean cotton.

1760
James Hargreaves invents the spinning jenny that spins thread into yarn.

1800
Alessandro Volta invents the battery.

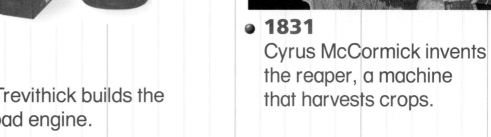

1804
Richard Trevithick builds the first railroad engine.

1831
Cyrus McCormick invents the reaper, a machine that harvests crops.

1844
Rubber is made strong enough to use.

1844
The telegraph is invented.

1807
Robert Fulton builds the first successful steamboat.

1844
Elias Howe invents the sewing machine.

1856
Henry Bessemer shows
how to make strong steel.

1861
Coast to coast communication in
the U.S.A. is made possible with
the telegraph.

1858
The first rubber eraser is put on the end
of a pencil.

1857
The passenger elevator is invented.

1861
Nicolaus August Otto makes
the first engine powered by gasoline.

1863
James Plimpton makes the
first set of roller skates.

1865
The first fax machines
are used.

1873
The typewriter
is invented.

1876
The first telephone call is made.

1884
The fountain pen is invented.

1884
The first roller coaster is built.

1885
The first car that uses gasoline is invented.

1877
The record player is invented.

1893
The zipper is invented.

1889
The first dishwasher is invented.

1896
George Washington Carver, a scientist, makes many products from peanuts.

1879
The light bulb is invented.

1902
William Carrier makes the first air conditioner.

1903
The first crayons are made.

1903
The Wright brothers fly the first airplane.

1920
Radio entertains millions of people in America.

1906
The first radio broadcast is heard.

1906
The first cartoon is made.

1907
Leo Baekeland invents plastic.

1913
The refrigerator is invented.

1925
Masking tape is invented.

1927
Philo Farnsworth demonstrates the first television.

1928
Sir Alexander Fleming discovers penicillin.

1930
Clarence Birdseye introduces frozen foods.

1931
The Empire State Building is built.

1940
Nylon is invented.

1941
Les Paul builds the first electric guitar.

1946
ENIAC, the first computer, is built.

1947
The microwave oven is invented.

1948
The telephone answering machine is invented.

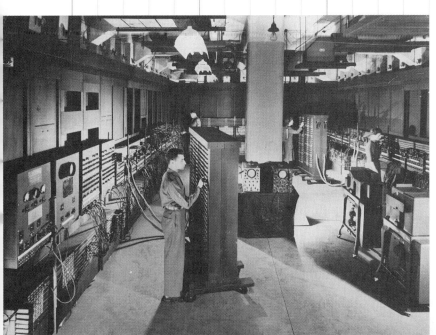

| 1950 | 1955 | 1960 | 1965 | 1970 |

1954
Color television is invented.

1957
The Soviet Union launches Sputnik, the first satellite into space.

1960
The photocopy machine is invented.

1961
Yuri Gagarin is the first man in space.

1964
Cassette tapes are invented.

1968
The first pair of running shoes is made.

1972
The first videotape machine is sold.

1974
The first bar codes appear in stores.

| 1975 | 1980 | 1985 | 1990 | 1995 – 2000 |

1981
The first space
shuttle is launched.

1975
The first personal
computer goes on sale.

1983
Cellular phone networking starts in the U.S.A.

1985
The first compact discs are sold.

1990
The Hubble Space
Telescope is launched.

1994
The Internet
becomes popular.

1998
John Glenn, age 77,
is the oldest person
to fly in space.

Glossary/Index

A

abdomen, A36, A44. The abdomen is a body part of an insect.

air, B10. Air is made of gases. People breathe air.

animal, A30. An animal is a living thing. Most animals can move around on their own. Animals eat plants or other animals.

aquarium, 33. An aquarium is a tank or glass bowl in which living fish, other water animals, and water plants are kept.

artery, 47. An artery is a tube in the body that carries blood away from the heart.

attract, B52, B60. Attract means to pull toward.

B

balance, D38. Balance means to stand without falling.

Big Dipper, C56. The Big Dipper is a group of stars that looks like a cup with a long handle.

blizzard, C39. A blizzard is a very strong snow storm.

blowhole, A55. A blowhole is a hole on top of a dolphin's head. Dolphins use a blowhole to breathe air.

bones, D29, D30. Bones are the hard part of the body. Bones hold the body up. Bones move when muscles pull them.

brain, 48. The brain is a part of the body that is inside the head. The brain controls the body. It helps people move, think, feel, and remember.

breathe, A55. To breathe is to take air into the lungs and then let it out.

C

cactus, A57. A cactus is a plant that usually has spines but no leaves. Most cactuses grow in very hot, dry places.

centimeter, B58. A centimeter is a unit for measuring length.

crosswalk, D42, D44. The white lines on the street that show the safest place to walk make up a crosswalk.

D

desert, A57. A desert is a dry place on the surface of the earth.

digestion, 46. The process of breaking down food is called digestion.

dinosaur, 37. A dinosaur is an extinct animal that lived millions of years ago. There were many different kinds of dinosaurs.

dissolve, 40. When something dissolves, it spreads evenly throughout a liquid.

dolphin, A55. A dolphin is a mammal that lives in the ocean. Dolphins use a blowhole on top of their heads to breathe air.

E

Earth, C48. Earth is the planet we live on. Earth is the third planet from the sun.

electric charge, 38, 39. Electric charges are the tiny bits of electricity in all matter.

electric circuit, 39. Electricity moves in a path called an electric circuit.

endangered, 30, 31. When a plant or animal is endangered, it means that very few are living.

esophagus, 46. The esophagus is the part of the body that squeezes food down to the stomach.

evaporates, B17. When water evaporates it changes into a gas called water vapor.

exercise, D36, D44. Playing and moving are ways to exercise.

F

feathers, A34. Feathers cover a bird's body.

flippers, A54. Flippers are wide, flat body parts that help some animals swim.

flood, C38. A flood is a large amount of water on land that is usually dry.

floss, D27. To floss is to clean between the teeth using a special kind of thread.

foam, B39. Foam is a lightweight material used to make cups and other things.

fog, C34. Fog is a cloud that is near the ground.

Food Guide Pyramid, D34, D44. The Food Guide Pyramid shows the food groups. It shows what foods to eat in order to stay healthy.

forest, A56. A forest is a large area covered with trees.

fossil, 36. A fossil is a part or print of a plant or animal that lived long ago.

freeze, B16. To freeze is to harden from cold. When water freezes, it turns into a solid.

fruit, A17, A20, A24. A fruit is the part of a plant where seeds are. An apple is a fruit.

fur, A34. Fur is the hair that covers some animals.

G

gas, B10, B20. Gas takes up space. It can change shape and size. Air is made of gases.

germs, D37. Germs are tiny living things. Some germs can make you sick.

gills, A55. Gills are the openings in the body that let fish breathe in the water.

globe, C17. A globe is a sphere with a map of Earth on it.

H

habitat, A52, A60. A habitat is a place where plants and animals live.

hail, C34. Hail is ice that falls from clouds.

hand lens, 53. A hand lens is a tool that makes objects look larger.

head, A36, A44. The head is a body part. It is one of the three main body parts of an insect.

heart, 47. The heart is the part of the body that pumps blood to other parts of the body.

hibernate, C43, C44. Hibernate means to spend the winter in a deep sleep.

I

insect, A36, A44. An insect is an animal that has three main body parts and six legs.

L

large intestine, 46. The large intestine is a part of the body. Food that is not digested goes into the large intestine. Then it passes out of the body as solid waste.

leaves, A12, A20, A24. Leaves are part of a plant. Leaves use light, air, and water to make food for the plant.

liquid, B8, B20. A liquid takes the shape of its container. Water is a liquid.

living things, A50, A60. Plants and animals are living things.

lungs, 47. Lungs are the part of the body that take in air.

M

machine, B56. A machine is a tool that makes work easier.

magnet, B52, B60. A magnet is an object that attracts some kinds of metal.

map, B48. A map is a drawing of a place. You can use a map to get from one place to another.

maze, B51. A maze is an area with many paths.

migrate, C42, C44. Migrate means to move from one place another when the seasons change. Some animals migrate to warm places in the winter.

mixture, 40. When two or more materials are mixed together, they form a mixture. The materials can easily be separated.

moon, C52. The moon is an object in the sky that moves around Earth.

mountain, C16. A mountain is a very large hill.

muscles, D28, D30. Muscles are a part of the body that help it move.

N

nerves, 48. Nerves are pathways in the body that carry messages to and from the brain.

nonliving things, A50, A60. Nonliving things cannot grow or move on their own.

O

object, B6, B20. An object is a thing you can see or touch.

observe, D6, D16. When you observe, you notice many things.

ocean, A54. The ocean is the large body of saltwater that covers much of the earth's surface.

Orion, C57. Orion is a group of stars that looks like a hunter wearing a belt.

oxygen, 47. Oxygen is a gas we need to breathe.

P

pan balance, 52. A pan balance is a tool used to measure mass. Mass is the amount of matter in an object.

parent, A42, A44. A parent is a mother or father.

phases, C53, C60. The shapes of the lighted part of the moon are called phases.

planet, 42, 43. A planet is a body of matter that moves around the sun.

plant, A8. A plant is any living thing that can make its own food from light, air, and water.

pull, B46, B60. A pull makes things move. When you put clothes away, you pull to open the drawer.

push, B46, B60. A push makes things move. To close the drawer, you push it shut.

R

recycle, C20, C22. Recycle means to take something that has been used and make something new from it.

repel, B52, B60. Repel means to push away.

reuse, C20, C22. Reuse means to use something again.

roots, A8, A20, A24. Roots are a part of a plant. Roots take in water and hold plants in the soil.

S

scales, A34. Scales are the hard plates that cover the bodies of some animals. Some fish, snakes, and lizards have scales.

sea turtle, A54. A sea turtle is a turtle that lives in the ocean.

sea urchin, A54. A sea urchin is a small animal that lives in the ocean. Sea urchins are covered with sharp spines.

season, C40, C44. A season is a time of the year. The seasons are spring, summer, fall, and winter.

seed, A14, A20, A24. A seed is a part of a plant that can grow into a new plant.

seed coat, A14. A seed coat is the outside layer that protects a seed.

senses, D10, D16. You use your senses to observe. The senses are seeing, hearing, smelling, touching, and tasting.

shadow, B30, B42. A shadow is made when something blocks the light.

shell, A34. A shell is a hard covering that protects some animals. Turtles have shells.

simple machine, B56, B60. A simple machine is a tool with few or no moving parts that makes work easier. A wheel and axle, inclined plane or ramp, lever, and pulley are four kinds of simple machines.

small intestine, 46. The small intestine is a part of the body that helps digest food. Most of the digestion happens in the small intestine.

soil, C12, C22. Soil is the top layer of the earth. Plants grow in soil.

solar system, 42, 43. The sun, the planets and their moons, and other objects that move around the sun form the solar system.

solid, B8, B20. A solid is an object that takes up space and has its own shape.

solution, 40. A solution is a mixture in which one material dissolves in another.

star, C56. A star is an object in the sky that gives off its own light.

stem, A8, A20, A24. The stem is the part of a plant that takes water and sugars to other parts of the plant and holds it upright.

stomach, 46. The stomach is a part of the body. Food is mixed in the stomach until it becomes liquid.

sun, C50. The sun is the star in the center of our solar system. All of the planets in our solar system move around the sun.

T

tadpole, A42. A tadpole is a very young frog or toad. Tadpoles have tails and live only in water.

teeth, D26. Teeth are used to bite and chew. Children usually get their first teeth before they are one year old. Permanent teeth replace first teeth later.

telescope, C52, C60. A telescope makes objects that are far away look closer.

temperature, C28, C44, 51. Temperature is how hot or cold something is.

terrarium, 32. A terrarium is a glass container in which plants or small land animals are kept.

thermometer, C32, C44, 51. A thermometer measures the temperature.

thorax, A36, A44. The thorax is a body part of an insect.

tornado, C39. A tornado is a very strong wind that comes down from the clouds in the shape of a funnel.

V

vein, 47. A vein is a tube in the body that carries blood to the heart.

vibrate, B26, B42. Vibrate means to move back and forth very fast.

W

water cycle, 41. The way water moves from the clouds to the earth and back to the clouds is called the water cycle.

water vapor, C34, C44. Water vapor is a form of water in the air. When liquid water evaporates, it changes to a gas called water vapor.

weathering, C8, C22. Wind, water, and ice can change rocks. This is called weathering.

wind, C30. Wind is moving air.

Acknowledgments

Illustration
Borders Patti Green
Icons Precison Graphics
Materials Icons Diane Teske Harris

Front Matter
iv T PhotoDisc, Inc.
iv B Walter Stuart
v B Artville
v B INS Tom McHugh/Photo Researchers
viii TL Dr. E.R. Degginer/Color-Pic, Inc.
viii TR Arthur Hill/Visuals Unlimited
ix T Adam Jones/Photo Researchers
ix B NASA
x T Marsha Winborn
x BL Telegraph Colour Library/FPG International
x BC Peter Correz/Tony Stone Images
x BR Phillip Engelhorn/Tony Stone Images

Unit A
4 Pauline Phung
8, 32b, 54 Walter Stuart
14 Rebecca Merrilees
16c Michael Carroll
26 Judy Moffatt
40 Tom Leonard
46 Marsha Winborn
48 Eileen Hine
52 Kristin Kest

Unit B
3 Hyewon Shin
4 Annie Lunsford
12, 13 Ginna Magee
17 Dara Goldman
20 Diane Teske Harris
22 Stacey Schuett
24, 36, 56, 60 Tom Leonard
33 Don Tate
38a Carol Stutz
44 Marshall Woksa
48, 49 Eileen Hine
55a Elizabeth Wolf

Unit C
4 Trudy L. Calvert
17c John Edwards
18b Diane Paterson
21a Precision Graphics
24a-c David Wenzel
26 Donna Nelson
32a Roger Roth
46 Walter Stuart
54, 55 Elizabeth Wolf
56 John Edwards

Unit D
4 Georgia C. Shola
16a Carol Stutz
18 Cristina Ventoso
27c Diane Teske Harris
28b, 29b John Edwards
32 Marsha Winborn
40, 41 Diane Paterson
42 Pauline Phung
36, 37 Robert Lawson

Photography
Unless otherwise credited, all photographs are the property of Scott Foresman, a division of Pearson Education. Page abbreviations are as follows: (T) top, (C) center, (B) bottom, (L) left, (R) right, (INS) inset.

Cover: Rick Iwasaki/Tony Stone Images

iv PhotoDisc, Inc.
v L Artville
v R Tom McHugh/Photo Researchers
viii T Dr. E. R. Degginger/Color-Pic, Inc.
viii B Arthur Hill/Visuals Unlimited
ix T Adam Jones/Photo Researchers
ix B NASA
x L Telegraph Colour Library/FPG International Corp.
x C Peter Correz/Tony Stone Images
x R Philipp Engelhorn/Tony Stone Images

Unit A
1 Jeff Hunter/Image Bank
2 C D. Demello/Wildlife Conservation Society headquartered at the Bronx Zoo
2 BL Greg Marshall/National Geographic
2 B-Background Pete Saloutos/Stock Market
2 T Vincent O'Bryne/Panoramic Images
16 L William J. Weber/Visuals Unlimited
16 R Joseph L. Fontenot/Visuals Unlimited
17 L William J. Weber/Visuals Unlimited
17 R Joyce Photographics/Photo Researchers
22 B David R. Frazier/Tony Stone Images
30 T Francois Gohier/Photo Researchers
30 BC PhotoDisc, Inc.
30 CC PhotoDisc, Inc.
30 BL PhotoDisc, Inc.
30 BR PhotoDisc, Inc.
32 Stephen Dalton/Photo Researchers
34 Tiger-Tom McHugh/Photo Researchers
34 Bluejay-Elvan Habicht/Animals Animals/Earth Scenes
34 Goldfish-George Bernard/Animals Animals/Earth Scenes
34 Turtle-Bill Beatty/Visuals Unlimited
34 Turtle shell-Maslowski/Visuals Unlimited
34 Tiger stripes-Tim Davis/Photo Researchers
34 Goldfish scales-G. I. Bernard/Animals Animals/Earth Scenes
34 Bluejay feathers-Thomas Martin/Photo Researchers
36 TR Artville
36 CL Artville
36 CR Artville
36 BR Leroy Simon/Visuals Unlimited
37 TL Artville
37 TR Leroy Simon/Visuals Unlimited
37 BCL Artville
37 BR Artville
37 BCR Artville
37 BL Artville
38 Artville
42 Anup & Manuj Shah//Animals Animals/Earth Scenes
43 TL E. R. Degginger/Color-Pic, Inc.
43 TC Stephen Dalton/Photo Researchers
43 TR Tom McHugh/Photo Researchers
50 T PhotoDisc, Inc.
50 C Rod Planck/Photo Researchers
50 BL Brock May/Photo Researchers
56 Background Doug Sokell/Visuals Unlimited
56 TR Joe McDonald/Visuals Unlimited
56 CL Leonard Lee Rue IV, NAS/Photo Researchers
56 BR Fred Unverhau/Animals Animals/Earth Scenes
57 Background Doug Sokell/Visuals Unlimited
57 TR C.K. Lorenz/Photo Researchers
57 CL Richard Kolar/Animals Animals/Earth Scenes
57 BR C.K. Lorenz/Photo Researchers

Unit B
1 A. Gin/Picture Perfect
2 B Sunny Cor Inc.
2 C Grantpix/Photo Researchers
2 T Vincent O'Bryne/Panoramic Images

Unit C
1 Chuck Szymanski/International Stock
2 B ESA/SPL/Photo Researchers
2 Inset-c Joseph Sohm/ChromoSohm/Corbis Media
2 C Royal Mat Inc.
2 T Vincent O'Bryne/Panoramic Images
3 CR NASA
3 CL NASA
8 L Dr. E.R. Degginger/Color-Pic, Inc.
8 C Dr. E. R. Degginger/Color-Pic, Inc.
8 R Arthur Hill/Visuals Unlimited
16 L Paul Chesley/Tony Stone Images
16 R Larry Ulrich/Tony Stone Images
17 L Tony Stone Images
17 R Dr. Ed Degginger/Bruce Coleman Inc.
28 B D. Young-Wolff/PhotoEdit
34 L Adam Jones/Photo Researchers
34 R Wendy Shattil/Bob Rozinski/TOM STACK & ASSOCIATES
35 L Doug Miller/Photo Researchers
35 R Joyce Photographics/Photo Researchers
38 ©Tom Stack & Associates/Wm. L. Wantland
39 L ©Tom Stack & Associates/Merrilee Thomas
39 R Aaron Strong
/Liaison Agency
40 TL Bill Beatty/Visuals Unlimited
40 TR Bill Beatty/Visuals Unlimited
40 BL Bill Beatty/Visuals Unlimited
40 BR Bill Beatty/Visuals Unlimited
42 John Gerlach/Visuals Unlimited
42 Inset Maslowski/Visuals Unlimited
43 L Lindholm/Visuals Unlimited
43 R Tom J. Ulrich/Visuals Unlimited
48 NASA
50 Eric R. Berndt/Unicorn Stock Photos
52 T John Bova/Photo Researchers
53 L John Bova/Photo Researchers
53 R John Bova/Photo Researchers
55 Photo Researchers
56 Royal Observatory Edinburgh/SPL/Photo Researchers

Unit D
1 William Sallaz/Duomo Photography Inc.
2 C Michael Newman/PhotoEdit
2 B Larry Mulvehill/Photo Researchers
2 T Vincent O'Bryne/Panoramic Images
3 B Myrleen Ferguson/Photo Edit/Picture Network International
8 Myrleen Ferguson/PhotoEdit
9 L Maresa Pryor/Animals Animals/Earth Scenes
9 R Lon Lauber/Alaska Stock
26 L Telegraph Colour Library/FPG International Corp.
26 C Peter Correz/Tony Stone Images
26 R Philipp Engelhorn/Tony Stone Images
27 Nancy Sheehan/PhotoEdit
34 Elizabeth Simpson/FPG International Corp.
36 R Michael Newman/PhotoEdit

End Matter

4 Bob Kalmbach, University of Michigan Photo Services
30 T Dan Suzio/Photo Researchers
30 BL Marianne Austin-McDermon
30 BR Paul M. Montgomery
31 TL Art Wolfe/Tony Stone Images
31 TR Gary Carter/Visuals Unlimited
31 B Dr. & TL Schrichte/Tony Stone Images
36 T A. J. Copley/Visuals Unlimited
36 BL Denver Museum of Natural History/Photo Researchers
36 BR E. R. Degginger/Color-Pic, Inc.
44 B NASA
45 NASA
56 T Cliff Hollenbeck/Tony Stone Images
56 B The Granger Collection, New York
57 T British Library
57 CL Ancient Art & Architecture Collection/Ronald Sheridan Photo-Library
57 CC Corbis Media
57 CR Culver Pictures Inc.
57 BL The Granger Collection, New York
58 T Drawing by F. M. Barber in 1885/Bushnell
58 CL Deutsches Museum
58 CR Smithsonian Institution
58 B Culver Pictures Inc.
59 TL Museo Nazionale Della Scienza & Della Tecnica Leonardo da Vinci Milan
59 TR Newell Convers Wyeth/International Harvester Company
59 CL Stock Montage
59 CR Stock Montage, Inc.
59 B Smithsonian Institution of Physical Sciences
60 C Otis Elevator Company
60 B Hagley Museum and Library
60 T Culver Pictures Inc.
61 TL Corbis Media
61 TR Culver Pictures Inc.
61 CR Corbis Media
61 BL General Electric
62 BL Karen M. Koblik
62 BR Corbis Media
63 T Corbis Media
63 C Public Domain
63 B University of Pennsylvania Libraries
64 T UPI/Corbis Media
64 CL UPI/Corbis Media
64 CR Corel
64 B William Whitehurst/Stock Market
65 TR NASA
65 TL Computer Museum, Boston
65 C PhotoDisc, Inc.
65 B NASA